More Freedom within a framework

Breathing new life into liturgy

TIM LOMAX

kevin
mayhew

First published in 2002 by
KEVIN MAYHEW LTD
Buxhall, Stowmarket
Suffolk IP14 3BW

9 8 7 6 5 4 3 2 1 0

ISBN 1 84003 940 X
Catalogue No. 1500527

Cover design by Jonathan Stroulger
Edited and typeset by Elisabeth Bates
Printed in Great Britain

Contents

Acknowledgements

I would dearly like to thank the following people. John Darch – for your excellent help with the book, ensuring that its focus was clear and used *Common Worship* to its full potential. John Witcombe, a true friend – it has been a privilege to serve and grow alongside you these past three years. The students and staff at St John's College, Nottingham, for all the worship, ideas and experiences we have shared. Graham and Stephen Knott and the people of St John's Church, Mansfield, for the year we have spent together in worship and service. John Leach and Jeremy Fletcher for your encouragement at the start of the *Freedom Within a Framework* book projects – you gave me the confidence and advice needed. Mike Moynagh for the input on 'Liquid Worship' plus the very enjoyable times of inspirational conversation we share together. Richard Lewis, a great friend and mentor from whom I learn so much about a genuine life of worship. Liz Bates – for being a great editor, taking the time to ensure that the text is comprehensible. Friends and family, particularly my mum and dad who offer support in so many wonderful ways. And most especially Katie. Your heart for God and his Church are a constant example to me. The love and encouragement you share never run dry; they are a true gift.

Foreword

'Give people a fish, and you feed them for a day,' went a Christian Aid slogan of a few years ago, 'Teach people to fish, and you feed them for life.' There are two problems which often go with books of resources: the first is that people simply swallow them, and the second is that they then regurgitate them messily.

Building on the clear success of his first *Freedom Within a Framework* Tim is very clear that neither of these things should happen with these worship outlines. They are, of course, resources which are easily usable as they stand, but his clear intention is not that we use them slavishly, but that they are 'catalysts . . . to spark life and to act as a tool'. His real aim is that as we are immersed in his material, we might develop the skills to invent our own. This book does contain some very good fish indeed, but it will be most helpful if we see it as a fishing manual.

But the thing I value most about Tim's material, and which I believe is his unique contribution, is that column down the right of the service outlines headed 'Directions'. It is possible to get the very best resource material and then make a doggie's breakfast out of it: Tim's extremely practical rubrics make plain to even the most liturgically challenged of worship leaders what is meant to happen, how and why. His concern is that worship flows smoothly without gaps or jars, and this 'stage-management' column really can ensure that this happens. Again, this could be seen just as a few fishy morsels, but is in reality a practical teaching tool for effective worship-leading.

But there are two further things I value about this book, and paradoxically they may seem to be opposed to each other. As in the previous book, and indeed as in the very title, Tim is concerned about that framework in which we can be free. His concern, like mine, is not that Anglican liturgy should somehow be made unnecessary by the coming of the Holy Spirit, but rather that like scaffolding it should support and strengthen what he is building among us. *Common Worship* provides a rich vein of resource for Spirit-led worship, and Tim has worked on material which values and takes seriously this liturgical tradition, rather than scrapping it in favour of a minimalist charismatic song-sandwich (often with very little meat indeed).

But at the same time Tim is concerned to push the boundaries, even beyond the latest offerings from the Liturgical Commission, and his final section on 'Liquid Worship', which many are sensing will be an important way forward, flags up the need for us constantly to reinvent worship in the context of a rapidly changing world. And yet we are still encouraged to use lectionary readings, a Eucharistic Prayer, the Peace, and so on. Even with this degree of freedom, the framework is very much in evidence.

So I hope that in many different ways this book will teach you to fish, and I hope too that among Anglicans who are either stuck in a rut or so much in the groove that they abandon their heritage, there will be a new reverence for the framework in which freedom can be most free.

JOHN LEACH

About the author

Tim Lomax is one of a new generation of worship leaders/songwriters who are being brought to the forefront of the contemporary worship scene in the twenty-first century. His driving passion is to reflect the One who won his heart to win the hearts of others.

Tim is now worship minister at St Mary's church, Luton, where his wife, Kate, serves as a curate. Until recently Tim co-ordinated the music for St John's College, Nottingham, whilst Kate studied there for the ordained ministry. He was also Worship Consultant for St John's Church, Mansfield. Tim's heart is to assist and equip forward-thinking churches who wish to move out of the repetitive cycle of traditional forms of worship into more contemporary and relevant styles, without losing or letting go of their rich heritage.

Tim's involvement with worship began when he was a teenager, joining his local church's music group as a keyboard player. After studying music and teaching at the University of Derby, he spent four years at St Andrew's and St Peter's, Weston Coyney, Stoke-on-Trent, as their Music Director, Worship Leader and Youth and Children's Worker. Such a broad scope of responsibility gave him experience in planning and leading worship, mission work, all-age worship, multimedia youth events, and schools work. During this period Tim married Kate, who at that time was a nurse in Stoke.

As part of his ministry Tim also leads worship, speaks and provides training for churches and conferences around the country. He is a member of GROW (group for the renewal of worship). His songs are published by world wide worship at Kevin Mayhew. He is director of the 'Fit for heaven?' worship conference and the 'Fit for heaven?' worship leader's network. He also heads up his worship band, lokate.

Tim's website: www.lokate-music.net

Introduction

This book builds on the concepts and ideas identified within *Freedom Within a Framework*. As well as being a sequel to the first book, *More Freedom Within a Framework*, as its name suggests, aims to help develop Anglican worship further so as to achieve even more freedom within a liturgical framework. More freedom by using slightly less formal liturgy, by using more of the liturgy variations provided within *Common Worship*, by encouraging further creativity, facilitating increased open worship that enables spontaneous expression, and by including more space in which we are open to the Holy Spirit influencing worship. To help achieve this, more scope is given to the user of the ready-made service outlines provided. Much less of the plans and ideas are prescribed or outlined in detail, giving more creative licence to the worship leader. For example, no formal written prayers are provided within the Intercession sections of the service outlines. These have been replaced by guidelines for intercessory worship and other creative options.

A set of 18 contemporary service outlines are provided in a ready-to-use format. These comprise nine Services of Holy Communion, three Services of the Word, four Services of the Word with Holy Communion, one Liquid Worship Service (explained later in the introduction) and one Service of Meditations on the Word. Within them written liturgies taken from *Common Worship*, music and creative ideas combine to facilitate a flowing journey of worship, response and openness to God. Use them in the light of the concepts and challenges highlighted within this introductory section to develop worship and spark innovation.

CD-ROM

An accompanying CD-ROM is provided. This contains ready-made Power-Point presentations for two of the services within the book (Easter Day Holy Communion and the Fifteenth Sunday after Trinity Holy Communion). Liturgies and images have been laid out creatively within each presentation. These can be projected onto a large screen using a computer and video/data projector, thus making all words required for the service accessible to the congregation in a creative and contemporary way. Each presentation can be amended and customised using PowerPoint software.

Why use this book?

Maybe you and your co-ministers are wondering how to achieve more freedom within a *Common Worship* framework. Perhaps you would like to develop the worship within your church so that there is more of a balance between truth and Spirit. You may wish to see more imaginative worship but lack the ideas, vision or time. Maybe you have identified spiritual needs in your congregation that could be met through the introduction of this type of worship. Alternatively, you may wish to broaden your horizons and understanding as a worship leader.

How do I use this book?

This book is designed as a user-friendly resource. It could act as a catalyst in the life of the church or in your own ministry. All the plans and ideas in this book are by no means set in stone. They are there simply to spark life and to act as a tool. So, feel free to use them as they are or to adapt them. In time it is my hope that you will be better equipped to invent your own.

Each service outline provides a detailed plan suitable for principal (main) Sunday worship. All are related to specific weeks in the lectionary year and can be used with the corresponding principal readings of all three *Common Worship* lectionary years. Each outline is accompanied by full instructions to guide you and your co-ministers through the worship. The guidelines are not intended to restrict the flow of worship or even to create a carefully choreographed piece of worship excellence. On the contrary, it is hoped that such structure gives way to freedom and encourages a smooth flow of worship. Song/hymn suggestions, worship components and other creative ideas can be followed, omitted or adapted in order to suit your own thoughts or style. Further artistic elements such as dance, drama, signing (as used for the deaf), images or artwork, can be added to each service where appropriate. Suggested songs and hymns are taken from the following books: *The Source, The Source 2, The Bridge, Release* and *Complete Anglican Hymns Old and New*, all of which are available from your local Christian book-shop or Kevin Mayhew Publishers (www.kevinmayhewltd.com).

How can we achieve more freedom within a framework?

By viewing liturgy as a restrictive cage we limit our worship and ourselves greatly. But if we see liturgy as scaffolding within which we add other essential components of worship then we will be free to build genuine worship, worship that is full of life. I find it exciting to think that by including more than just the usual hymn slots, readings and sermon, worship can be transformed.

The following components can help build worship that is full of life (these are discussed in more detail within *Freedom Within a Framework*):

A desire to see the Holy Spirit impacting worship

An openness to see the Holy Spirit active within worship (inspiring our understanding of the word, bringing personal and corporate growth and renewal, healing, empowering with gifts of the Spirit). We can make Spirit-impacted worship our heart's desire and pray earnestly for God to move among us in power.

Praise

When we gather together as congregations to praise Almighty God we join with all of heaven and earth. There is nothing greater than praising the Lord – it is good and fitting.

Adoration

The underlying aim of all services is to worship God, to give him his worth ('worship' = 'worth-ship'). Adoration is defined as the act of worshipping.

When we draw close to God and stay in his presence our desire is to adore him, expressing our intense admiration and offering our deep love for him.

Intimacy

Having drawn close enough to bow at the feet of the Lord and adore him we are now close enough to kiss him. In his presence we are aware not only of our sinfulness but also that we are forgiven. Jesus has given us so much. His love for us is vast and we are overcome with gratitude and admiration. Our response – to love him unreservedly and to enjoy the intimate relationship he encourages.

Reflection

Worship should include time for us to think, meditate and ponder in God's presence. This can be done by introducing space for people to use how they wish; e.g. to think upon God's character or his love, to meditate on his word or as the hymn expresses so beautifully to 'ponder anew what the Almighty can do'.

Silence

The simple response to God's glory in our midst is reverent silence. Not because we show reverence by being silent but because when we truly know that we are in the presence of God we can be lost for words and want to remain still and quiet. By including silence within worship we can also encourage congregations to listen to God and be open to receiving gifts of the Spirit that can be expressed afterwards (e.g. prophecy, tongues).

Response to God's word

God's word requires a response. We should be listeners and doers. This means that to conclude the Liturgy of the Word we ought to give space for a response process to start, e.g. commitment, repentance, seeking healing or forgiveness, prayer.

Music and liturgy flowing together

By blending liturgy and sung worship as in the service plans provided, much of our worship can move in an unbroken flow. Instead of using isolated hymns or songs in between certain elements of liturgy, instrumental music (played by music group or organ) can link songs and provide a backdrop for the spoken word. At appropriate points the music can lead into the singing of hymns or songs. It is also possible to split a hymn or song with an element of liturgy.

Open worship

Times of open worship can be used simply to encourage openness to aspects of worship not included in a formal liturgy. Within them people can be free to express their praise or prayers spontaneously. Space may be given for testimonies and in some churches the sharing of spiritual gifts including prophecy, singing in the Spirit, speaking in tongues or words of knowledge.

Extended times of sung worship

Instead of singing one song or hymn, a number of them can be linked to form an extended time of sung worship. Put simply, worship is a journey. Times of sung worship can help us travel some of this journey. A collection of well-chosen hymns and songs can lead us through certain aspects of worship.

e.g. Praise → Adoration → Intimacy → Reflection/Silence

Intercession

If prayers are to be truly 'of the people' we ought to include a little more freedom within the intercession liturgy. This can help ensure that the whole congregation are more engaged in prayer. The service outlines in this book encourage more freedom, creativity and spontaneity within the intercessions. In some of the service plans headings and/or visual stimuli are used to inspire prayer whilst space is provided to encourage people to offer their own prayers either silently or aloud. In others intercessory worship is encouraged in which sung worship provides the framework for or leads into prayer. A song/hymn (or part of one) is used as a refrain during the intercessions. For example – a song reflecting a prayerful theme can be sung in full before giving way to open prayer (spontaneous personal prayers offered silently or aloud from members of the congregation). The chorus of the song can then be used to conclude each prayer section. Prayers can be directed by headings projected onto a screen. Alternatively, a prayer leader can say spontaneous or written prayers whilst leaving space for open prayer. In some churches this form of worship may lead to the sharing of prophecies and other spiritual gifts. Some gifted musicians or members of the congregation may be able to sing prayers, prophecies or passages of scripture. Projected images, artwork, dance and signing could also be used creatively within this section of the service.

Prayer ministry

All main times of church worship ought to include opportunity for prayer ministry. It is one of the ways in which a church looks after the spiritual and physical welfare of its members. By making it available at appropriate times within the service people have the chance to ask for prayer and make their requests to God with the help of others. It also means that they can deal with issues highlighted during the worship. In addition churches can pray for those with specific ministries or those who are about to embark on them.

Freedom of expression

The Holy Spirit releases us in worship to express our hearts unreservedly. He enables us to worship with our whole being – body, mind and spirit. The Bible is littered with examples of how worship can be offered. Therefore, in addition to the expressions of worship contained within written liturgy it is important that we actively encourage people to enjoy the freedom of expression that the Holy Spirit brings – movement (e.g. clapping, raising hands), sharing gifts of the Spirit and spontaneous expression (aloud or private) – this can be to offer prayers, truths about God, testimony, proclamation, praise, thanks or lamentation.

Creativity

Creativity brings innovation and dynamism to worship. It can also bring relevance to each church in its local setting. It is something we ought to desire and facilitate in services as much as possible.

The following can help. *Music* – combining liturgy with music, inspiring background music to elements of worship, ministry songs (sung or played to the congregation). *Visual elements* – images, artwork, video material, symbols, banners, flags, icons, candles. *Practical responses/rituals*, e.g. committing yourself to Christ by placing your thumbprint on a cross. *Animated liturgy* (liturgy that is done as opposed to said). *Drama, meditation, movement, creative prayer, setting* – a stimulating worship environment and taste, touch and smell.

The type of worship highlighted in this book aims to build the above components into a creative liturgy framework.

The following areas concerning worship, when addressed, can also help achieve more freedom within a framework:

Evolving worship

Because formal liturgies have historically remained unchanged for long periods of time within the Anglican Church, poor use of liturgy has developed and in many cases services have become staid and repetitious. For many churches the only things that change from week to week are the readings, sermon and hymns. And because liturgy is used as the primary expression of worship, and not as a framework, little gets added to (or taken from) the service. For these reasons worship is prevented from evolving. True worship grows and develops with the journey and life of individuals and a church. It should never be encouraged to stand still. We need to plan worship that facilitates the opportunities for life-changing encounters with God. We should desire and work for worship that increasingly meets the spiritual needs of the congregation so that our lives of worship evolve corporately and individually.

It has also been said that services should reflect the object of our worship. By looking at many of our services does this mean that God is dull, boring and lifeless? Not at all! He is anything but those things. We should be inspired to continually develop services that more truly reflect the dynamism and creativity of the one whom we worship. Acts of worship should mirror and open the door to the splendour of God. Genuine worship fills our vision with his amazing character and attributes. So then, worship should be packed not just with formal words but with an array of dynamic, relevant, meaningful elements (old and new) that communicate God's splendour.

Contemporary v old

Some churches believe that a youth worker is the answer to the problem of getting more young people into services. Similarly, other churches apparently think that simply by inviting newcomers along to services they become a 'seeker-friendly' church. These can only ever be parts of the answer. If young people are to attend services the style and form of *worship* must be appropriate to them. And, if we are to invite non-Christians to services then we must ensure that the *worship* is 'seeker-friendly'. Contemporary worship can help address the need for youth- and seeker-friendly worship. However, in addition there is still a need to develop and renew our worship so that it is relevant and meaningful to *all* – church members and seekers, adults and young people. We must begin to facilitate worship that connects with today's people. Creativity is a tool which can contemporise worship and help make it more accessible. Artistic styles of the day, modes of communication, technology and the latest styles of music can all be used to bring worship to life and life to worship. Presentations and performances can communicate the gospel and creative ideas can be employed to stimulate the mind, heart and senses in worship. Inspirational worship environments can be created in which the spoken words provide the framework for dynamic, meaningful services. *But* it is important that we contemporise services without losing our rich heritage of worship, meaningful traditions and a sense of awe and wonder in God's presence. New worship elements should never be selected purely for their contemporary style. Otherwise we run the risk of selecting content which is very trendy but has little truth or worship value. In bringing contemporary elements to services and popularising worship we should be careful not to water down the content and meaning. Similarly, traditional worship elements should never be included in worship simply because they always have been. Every part of a service should be relevant, meaningful and accessible.

Worship that effectively combines the best of both the old and new will strike a healthy balance between material brought with us from the past and contemporary components which will help take the church into the future.

The best of the old

We can build into services wonderful expressions of worship that have been handed down to us. Often timeless truths are wrapped up in beautiful resources of faith that shine just as brilliantly now as they did in years gone by. Traditional hymns often encapsulate sentiments and meaning that we would otherwise struggle to communicate. Some expressions of faith have been passed down from the early church in the first centuries AD and many of these are contained within formal prayers still used today in the Anglican Church. Written liturgies (formal worship patterns) have also evolved over the centuries and they include many meaningful traditions that engage the heart and express faith practically.

It is important to remember that none of the above elements of worship carry merit merely for being old and established within the church. They should be included in services for one reason only – because they are an effective medium for offering worship to God. Now, this reason is open to debate, as you have probably found in your own church! Worship must be relevant in order for it to be offered genuinely from the heart to God. Our worship is restricted if we cannot relate to what we are being asked to express. One of the many beauties of worship is that it can communicate timeless truths to and of God in a contemporary manner. We can connect with and make use of the everyday things of the age in which we live to create worship that is relevant and meaningful. If we neglect this, worship can appear out of date, out of touch and irrelevant even though it may be packed full of truths and profound expressions of faith. We ought to remember that most people are used to pop music, computer games, the Internet and videos/DVDs. Almost all of us experience multimedia sound- and site-bites. Therefore, we can adapt church worship so that it connects with the life experiences of most people. When planning worship ask yourself the question – would most people (not church people) connect with this hymn, prayer and tradition or the style in which it is done? We should try to ensure then that services enable all people to glorify God in accessible, engaging and user-friendly ways. If someone walked into your church off the street would they easily pick up on all that was going on? This question is well worth consideration.

This means that planners of worship ought to select from the best of the 'old' resources available (hymns, traditions, formal liturgies and prayers). Obviously opinions and tastes differ so here are a few criteria to consider:

- Traditions (e.g. rituals) included within worship should be meaningful for all people present, should engage the heart and glorify God alone.
- Hymns ought to be user-friendly (easy to sing and understand), versatile (suitable for contemporary musical arrangements) and attractive to the congregation.
- Prayers should also be user-friendly (easy to read and understand) and suitable for additional creative ideas (e.g. visual elements).

One of the most effective ways to employ the best of the 'old' material is to give it a contemporary style. Traditional elements are then more likely to connect with the congregation. There are various ways to do this. Here are some ideas –

- Include traditional elements within a mainly contemporary framework that includes innovative material and ideas.
- Arrange hymns in a contemporary style (e.g. music group, band or piano arrangements – a drum or percussion rhythm helps).
- Combine traditional elements (e.g. confession, written prayers and rituals) with contemporary background music (live or recorded).
- Include innovative visual ideas (signing, dance, symbols, art, photographs, video material, computer-generated images) alongside more traditional elements.

The best of the new

Here and now elements of worship will help make our services contemporary, relevant and meaningful today – new songs, prayers, creative ideas, modern music and new technology. Such resources help to ensure that: worshippers relate to all the content and participate fully; all components of worship are easily accessible to everyone; worship is user-friendly; worship is a stimulating and inspirational encounter with God; and worship is creative and continually refreshed.

The last of these points I believe is the most crucial if we are to build worship that includes the best of the new. For this to happen we should set out to be creative and desire our worship to be constantly updated. God is creative and his Spirit brings creativity so that we in turn are free to express our faith and praises in imaginative, experiential ways.

When we seek to create worship using the best of the new we will find that we are actually building towards the future instead of holding onto the past. As God's people we should be looking to move forwards, asking God to do a new thing within his church. When we employ innovative material, resources, styles and ideas we demonstrate our passion for moving on looking to the church of tomorrow.

So, how do you select from the best of the new? Here are some suggestions to help:

- Only choose material that you think is sound. Unlike traditional material new ideas and resources have not stood the test of time. All material should be strong on truth and worship value, so if in doubt leave it out.
- New material and ideas should be meaningful and accessible for *all* people present, should engage the heart and glorify God alone.
- All new material should be user-friendly and easy to engage with.
- New material should help create a worshipful environment in which we encounter God. If it does not help to achieve this goal then it is not worth having.
- Include new material because of spiritual benefits not to be 'modern'.

*Liquid Worship**

This celebrates freedom in worship by catering for the differences that exist between individuals within a congregation. When we meet together we all come with different experiences of the week (or the day), different longings and different promptings from God. We may long to be quiet, we may long to be stimulated, we may have a burden to intercede, we may feel prompted to encounter God through an extended period of musical worship or we may feel led to receive prayer ministry. We may want to learn by listening, or we may find it easier to learn by discussing. Some may be new Christians still wanting a basic introduction to the faith, others may be 'old-stagers' seeking to explore their faith in more depth. Are there ways for corporate worship to take account of this diversity?

'Liquid Worship' gives worshippers more choice without losing the corporate dimension of worship. For instance every now and again, depending on the space and resources available, two or three different 'sermons' might be offered at the same time, such as one in a traditional mode, one involving a discussion and one making use of video. All three might be on different subjects.

Instead of everyone praying together in the same way during a church prayer meeting, there might be three or four different prayer stations in different parts of the building – one for intercessory prayer, for instance, one for prayer using visual images, one specifically for prayer ministry and one for silent prayer with Taizé music playing. Individuals could move round the various stations at their own pace or stay in one place for the whole meeting, and then come together at the end for a brief corporate act of worship and fellowship over refreshments.

* This section (see page 124) was written by Mike Moynagh of St John's College, Nottingham, and inspired by a conversation with Pete Ward in December 2000. For Pete's more radical proposals, see 'Liquid Church' – an interview with him in *Christianity and Renewal*, July 2001.

Taking the idea further, a whole service could be constructed around different stations. In the main building you might have a corporate act of worship led by musicians. In various rooms you might have different forms of prayer and two or three versions of the sermon slot, on the lines just described. These activities would continue throughout the 'service'. Worshippers could move between the venues in their own time, staying in any one as long as they wished. At the end everyone might come together for a short celebration of Communion and some refreshments.

This approach to worship respects the uniqueness of individuals. Someone who has recently been bereaved may find a period of corporate praise unhelpful, and prefer to spend the time in quiet prayer. Adult educators recognise that people have different learning styles, and it may be helpful for the church to acknowledge this too. Might liquid worship be more inclusive because it takes more account of diversity? Very different people may be more willing to come together because their individual needs are better catered for. An experiment here at St John's, Nottingham, suggested that older children and teenagers could find this fluid approach more attractive than traditional forms of all-age worship.

Liquid Worship can also enhance fellowship. When we gather as a single congregation, we may do the same thing together but there is not much communication between us. We sit in rows looking at the necks in front! But if people move between venues, there may be scope for brief conversations as they walk from one to the other. Certainly their different experiences of worship can become a topic of conversation over tea and coffee at the end – 'how did you spend most of your time this morning?'

Not least, liquid worship may be more in tune with our increasingly fluid culture. Today people are more likely to have flexible rather than fixed careers, relationships are more fluid with higher rates of separation and divorce, organisations are becoming more flexible in how they treat people (with products increasingly being customised to the individual, for example), and attitudes are less fixed by social and class backgrounds: attitudes may change quite radically during a person's life. The sociologist Zygmunt Bauman suggests that we are moving from a 'solid' to 'liquid modernity'.*

Yet church by and large feels stuck in the solid age. We meet at the same time every Sunday in the same place. We sit in fixed rows, whether pews or chairs, often in the same places every week. We tend to follow a fixed order of service. We all stand up and sit down at the same time. The sermon is roughly the same length every week – and we can't interrupt!

Some parts of society will always remain relatively 'solid' and so 'solid church' will always have a place. But just as Jesus immersed himself in the culture of his day in order to reach people, so too there may be a need for more fluid expressions of worship if today's church is to connect with the emerging liquid culture. To do this would not be a complete break from tradition. In Eastern European Orthodox churches it is not unusual for people to come and go through the service. Perhaps we can learn from them as we seek more fluid patterns of worship to serve the twenty-first century.

* Zygmunt Bauman, *Liquid Modernity*, Polity, 2000.

Service outlines

First Sunday of Advent
Service of Holy Communion

Order of Service

1 **Welcome and Notices**

2 **Introduction**

Stand

3 **Prayer of Preparation**

> **Almighty God,**
> **to whom all hearts are open,**
> **all desires known,**
> **and from whom no secrets are hidden:**
> **cleanse the thoughts of our hearts**
> **by the inspiration of your Holy Spirit,**
> **that we may perfectly love you,**
> **and worthily magnify your holy name;**
> **through Christ our Lord.**
> **Amen.**

Listen! You watchmen lift up your voices; together they shout for joy. When the Lord returns to Zion, they will see it with their own eyes. Burst into songs of joy together, you ruins of Jerusalem, for the Lord has comforted his people, and he has redeemed Jerusalem. The Lord will lay bare his holy arm in the sight of all the nations and all the ends of the earth will see the salvation of our God. Isaiah 52:8-10

4 **Extended time of Sung Worship**

Songs Bless the Lord, O my soul (*The Source 2*)
       He is the Lord (*The Source*)
Hymn O come, O come, Emmanuel
       (*Complete Anglican Hymns Old & New*)
Song Every knee shall bow – Chorale from 'Here is the
       risen Son' (*The Source 2*)

5 **Open Worship**

(Open to God, open prayer or praise, reflecting, sharing gifts of the Spirit)

6 **Silence**

Sit if not already doing so.

7 **Confession**

> When the Lord comes,
> he will bring to light the things now hidden in darkness,

Directions

Warm and inviting. Visitors and newcomers should be made particularly welcome.

A clear verbal outline of the service could be given.
SHORT PAUSE

Musical introduction to 'Bless the Lord, O my soul' begins as the scripture reading starts.

After the passage of scripture move directly into sung praise and worship.

Songs linked with instrumental music.

Sensitive instrumental music continues in the background. Open to the Holy Spirit. It may be appropriate to encourage the congregation to be free in their expression of worship at this point (e.g. to speak out prayer/praise or to pray silently). It is important for the worship leader to direct worship sensitively at this point.

Music ends.

and will disclose the purposes of the heart.
Therefore in the light of Christ let us confess our sins.

Almighty God, our heavenly Father,
we have sinned against you
and against our neighbour
in thought and word and deed,
through negligence, through weakness,
through our own deliberate fault.
We are truly sorry
and repent of all our sins.
For the sake of your Son Jesus Christ,
who died for us,
forgive us all that is past
and grant that we may serve you
in newness of life
to the glory of your name.
Amen.

Almighty God,
who forgives all who truly repent,
have mercy upon *you*,
pardon and deliver *you* from all *your* sins,
confirm and strengthen *you* in all goodness,
and keep *you* in life eternal;
through Jesus Christ our Lord.
Amen.

8 *Collect*

Silence

Almighty God,
give us grace to cast away the works of darkness
and to put on the armour of light,
now in the time of this mortal life,
in which your Son Jesus Christ came to us
in great humility;
that on the last day,
when he shall come again in his glorious majesty
to judge the living and the dead,
we may rise to the life immortal;
through him who is alive and reigns with you,
in the unity of the Holy Spirit,
one God, now and for ever.
Amen.

Song Every knee shall bow (refrain)

9 *The Liturgy of the Word*

Reading 1
Short time of silence

Gospel Reading
Alleluia, alleluia.
Prepare the way of the Lord, make his paths straight,
and all flesh shall see the salvation of God.
Alleluia.

Towards the end of the Collect a musical introduction to the song 'Every knee shall bow' begins.

Music ends.

The reading follows unannounced.

Inspirational images could be projected onto a screen to accompany the readings.

When the Gospel is announced the reader says
> Hear the Gospel of our Lord Jesus Christ according to N.
> **Glory to you, O Lord.**

Following the Gospel the reader says
> This is the Gospel of the Lord.
> **Praise to you, O Christ.**

Short time of silence

Sermon

Sermon linked to the overall theme if there is one. Challenging and affirming, giving practical help for discipleship. Contemporary and relevant, linking with everyday life, using illustrations, stories and imagery.

Silence

Silence used to reflect on the Sermon.

10 *Reflection and Response*

A song to minister. A song to listen to (recorded or performed live).

Suggestions Immanuel (Michael Card – *The Life* or *The Promise* albums)

I want to be in the light (D.C. Talk – *Jesus Freak* album)

Light of the world (Matt Redman – *The Father's Heart* album)

You bring me joy (Eden's Bridge – *All in a Life* album)

To facilitate reflection and/or response to the Sermon. An appropriate image could also be projected onto the screen. Mime or dance could be performed with the song.

11 *Open Prayer*

(Guided prayers offered by the congregation either silently or aloud)

Guidelines given regarding prayer topics through a prayer leader or OHP headings. The congregation can be encouraged to express prayers freely and as they feel comfortable (e.g. out loud or silently). At a certain point the congregation could be invited to speak out prayers simultaneously. The congregation could also be split into groups for prayer.

- Prayer for the world
- Prayer for this country
- Prayer for the wider church
- Prayer for our own church
- Prayer for our community
- Prayer for those in need
- Prayer for the lost

After a short pause the prayers follow unannounced.

Music (live or recorded) could be played in the background to the prayers. Projected images or artwork could also be used creatively. In some churches this form of open prayer may lead to the sharing of prophecies and other spiritual gifts.

Stand

12 *The Nicene Creed*

> **We believe in one God,**
> **the Father, the Almighty,**
> **maker of heaven and earth,**

of all that is,
seen and unseen.
**We believe in one Lord, Jesus Christ,
the only Son of God,
eternally begotten of the Father,
God from God,
Light from Light,
true God from true God,
begotten, not made,
of one Being with the Father;
through him all things were made.
For us and for our salvation
he came down from heaven,
was incarnate from the Holy Spirit
and the Virgin Mary
and was made man.
For our sake he was crucified under Pontius Pilate;
he suffered death and was buried.
On the third day he rose again
in accordance with the Scriptures;
he ascended into heaven
and is seated at the right hand of the Father.
He will come again in glory
to judge the living and the dead,
and his kingdom will have no end.**

**We believe in the Holy Spirit,
the Lord, the giver of life,
who proceeds from the Father and the Son,
who with the Father and the Son
is worshipped and glorified,
who has spoken through the prophets.
We believe in one holy catholic and apostolic Church.
We acknowledge one baptism
for the forgiveness of sins.
We look for the resurrection of the dead,
and the life of the world to come.
Amen.**

13 *The Peace*

In the tender mercy of our God,
the dayspring from on high shall break upon us,
to give light to those who dwell in darkness
and in the shadow of death
and to guide our feet into the way of peace.

The peace of the Lord be always with you
and also with you.

Let us offer one another a sign of peace.

All may exchange a sign of peace.

Song Through days of rage and wonder (*The Source 2*)

At an appropriate point following The Peace the music introduction to the song 'Through days of rage and wonder' begins.

14 *Eucharistic Prayer (F)*

The Lord be with you
and also with you.

Lift up your hearts.
We lift them to the Lord.

Let us give thanks to the Lord our God.
It is right to give thanks and praise.

You are worthy of our thanks and praise,
Lord God of truth,
for by the breath of your mouth
you have spoken your word,
and all things have come into being.

You fashioned us in your image
and placed us in the garden of your delight.
Though we chose the path of rebellion
you would not abandon your own.

Again and again you drew us
into your covenant of grace.
You gave your people the law
and taught us by your prophets
to look for your reign of justice, mercy and peace.

As we watch for the signs of your kingdom on earth,
we echo the song of the angels in heaven,
evermore praising you and *saying:*

Holy, holy, holy Lord,
God of power and might,
heaven and earth are full of your glory.
Hosanna in the highest.
[Blessed is he who comes in the name of the Lord.
Hosanna in the highest.]

Lord God, you are the most holy one,
enthroned in splendour and light,
yet in the coming of your Son Jesus Christ
you reveal the power of your love
made perfect in our human weakness.

Amen. Lord, we believe.

Embracing our humanity,
Jesus showed us the way of salvation;
loving us to the end,
he gave himself to death for us;
dying for his own,
he set us free from the bonds of sin,
that we might rise and reign with him in glory.

Amen. Lord, we believe.

On the night he gave up himself for us all
he took bread and gave you thanks;
he broke it and gave it to his disciples, saying:
Take, eat; this is my body which is given for you;
do this in remembrance of me.

Amen. Lord, we believe.

In the same way, after supper
he took the cup and gave you thanks;
he gave it to them, saying:
Drink this, all of you; this is my blood of the new covenant
which is shed for you and for many
for the forgiveness of sins.
Do this, as often as you drink it, in remembrance of me.

Amen. Lord, we believe.

Therefore we proclaim the death that he suffered
on the cross,
we celebrate his resurrection, his bursting from the tomb,
we rejoice that he reigns at your right hand on high
and we long for his coming in glory.

Amen. Come, Lord Jesus.

As we recall the one, perfect sacrifice of our redemption,
Father, by your Holy Spirit let these gifts of your creation
be to us the body and blood of our Lord Jesus Christ;
form us into the likeness of Christ
and make us a perfect offering in your sight.

Amen. Come, Holy Spirit.

Look with favour on your people
and in your mercy hear the cry of our hearts.
Bless the earth,
heal the sick,
let the oppressed go free
and fill your Church with power from on high.

Amen. Come, Holy Spirit.

Gather your people from the ends of the earth
to feast with [N and] all your saints
at the table in your kingdom,
where the new creation is brought to perfection
in Jesus Christ our Lord;
by whom, and with whom, and in whom,
in the unity of the Holy Spirit,
all honour and glory be yours, almighty Father,
for ever and ever.
Amen.

Song Through days of rage and wonder (vv 1 and 2)

15 *The Lord's Prayer*

**Our Father in heaven,
hallowed be your name,
your kingdom come,
your will be done,
on earth as in heaven.
Give us today our daily bread.
Forgive us our sins
as we forgive those who sin against us.
Lead us not into temptation
but deliver us from evil.
For the kingdom, the power, and the glory are yours
now and for ever.
Amen.**

On the words 'Gather your people' a clear musical introduction to the song 'Through days of rage and wonder begins'.

Music ends.

16 *Breaking of the Bread*

The president breaks the consecrated bread.

Every time we eat this bread
and drink this cup,
**we proclaim the Lord's death
until he comes.**

17 *Giving of Communion*

The president says the invitation to Communion

God's holy gifts
for God's holy people.
**Jesus Christ is holy,
Jesus Christ is Lord,
to the glory of God the Father.**

**Most merciful Lord,
your love compels us to come in.
Our hands were unclean,
our hearts were unprepared;
we were not fit
even to eat the crumbs from under your table.
But you, Lord, are the God of our salvation,
and share your bread with sinners.
So cleanse and feed us
with the precious body and blood of your Son,
that he may live in us and we in him;
and that we, with the whole company of Christ,
may sit and eat in your kingdom.
Amen.**

The president and people receive Communion.

Songs I am yours (*The Source 2*)
You are my King (*The Source*)
This is the air I breathe (*The Source 2*)
You are beautiful beyond description (*The Source*)

18 *Prayer after Communion*

Silence

O Lord our God,
make us watchful and keep us faithful
as we await the coming of your Son our Lord;
that, when he shall appear,
he may not find us sleeping in sin
but active in his service
and joyful in his praise;
through Jesus Christ our Lord.

**Almighty God,
we thank you for feeding us
with the body and blood of your Son Jesus Christ.
Through him we offer you our souls and bodies
to be a living sacrifice.
Send us out in the power of your Spirit
to live and work to your praise and glory.
Amen.**

Songs linked with instrumental music.

Prayer ministry could be made available at an appropriate place within the church during Communion.

Music ends.

Stand
Song We have sung our songs of victory (*The Source 2*)

19 *The Blessing and Dismissal*

Christ the Sun of Righteousness shine upon you,
scatter the darkness from before your path,
and make you ready to meet him when he comes in glory;
and the blessing of God almighty,
the Father, the Son, and the Holy Spirit,
be among you and remain with you always.
Amen.

Go in peace to love and serve the Lord.
In the name of Christ. Amen.

20 *Prayer Ministry Available*

The final song is announced.

Before the blessing and dismissal inform the congregation that prayer ministry is available after the service.

Soft worship music could be played or sung as people leave or as prayer continues.

First Sunday of Epiphany
Service of the Word with Holy Communion

Order of Service

1 **Welcome and Notices**

2 **Introduction**

Stand

3 **Extended Time of Sung Worship**

Hymn O worship the Lord in the beauty of holiness
(*The Source*)
Song Come, let us worship Jesus (*The Source*)
Song King of kings, majesty (*The Source*)

4 **Open Worship**

(Open to God, open prayer or praise, reflecting, sharing
gifts of the Spirit, sharing testimony)

Silence

5 **Confession**

Sit if not already doing so.

Song The giver of grace (*Release*)

Let us confess our sins.

**Father eternal, giver of light and grace,
we have sinned against you
and against our neighbour,
in what we have thought,
in what we have said and done,
through ignorance, through weakness,
through our own deliberate fault.
We have wounded your love
and marred your image in us.
We are sorry and ashamed
and repent of all our sins.
For the sake of your Son Jesus Christ,
who died for us,
forgive us all that is past
and lead us out from darkness
to walk as children of light.
Amen.**

May the Father of all mercies
cleanse *us* from *our* sins,

Directions

Warm and inviting. Visitors and newcomers
should be made particularly welcome.

A clear verbal outline of the service could
be given.

Songs linked using instrumental music.

Sensitive instrumental music continues in
the background. Open to the Holy Spirit.
It may be appropriate to encourage the
congregation to be free to worship as they
feel led at this point (e.g. to speak out
prayer/praise or to pray silently). It is
important for the worship leader to direct
worship sensitively at this point.

Music ends.

Soft background music continues during
the Confession.

Towards the end of the Absolution the
background music develops into a clear
introduction to the song 'The giver of grace'.

and restore *us* in his image
to the praise and glory of his name,
through Jesus Christ our Lord.
Amen.

Song The giver of grace (chorus)

6 *The Peace*

Our Saviour Christ is the Prince of Peace.
Of the increase of his government and of peace
there shall be no end.

The peace of the Lord be always with you
and also with you.

Let us offer one another a sign of peace.

All may exchange a sign of peace.

7 *Eucharistic Prayer (E)*

The Lord be with you
and also with you.

Lift up your hearts.
We lift them to the Lord.

Let us give thanks to the Lord our God.
It is right to give thanks and praise.

All honour and praise be yours always and everywhere,
mighty creator, ever-living God,
through Jesus Christ your only Son our Lord:
for at this time we celebrate your glory
made present in our midst.
In the coming of the Magi
the King of all the world was revealed to the nations.
In the waters of baptism
Jesus was revealed as the Christ,
the Saviour sent to redeem us.
In the water made wine
the new creation was revealed at the wedding feast.
Poverty was turned to riches, sorrow into joy.
Therefore with all the angels of heaven
we lift our voices to proclaim the glory of your name
and sing our joyful hymn of praise:

Holy, holy, holy Lord,
God of power and might,
heaven and earth are full of your glory.
Hosanna in the highest.
[Blessed is he who comes in the name of the Lord.
Hosanna in the highest.]

We praise and bless you, loving Father,
through Jesus Christ, our Lord;
and as we obey his command,
send your Holy Spirit,
that broken bread and wine outpoured
may be for us the body and blood of your dear Son.

Music ends.

The Eucharistic Prayer follows on from the Peace as soon as possible.

On the night before he died he had supper with his friends
and, taking bread, he praised you.
He broke the bread, gave it to them and said:
Take, eat; this is my body which is given for you;
do this in remembrance of me.

When supper was ended he took the cup of wine.
Again he praised you, gave it to them and said:
Drink this, all of you;
this is my blood of the new covenant,
which is shed for you and for many
for the forgiveness of sins.
Do this, as often as you drink it, in remembrance of me.

So, Father, we remember all that Jesus did,
in him we plead with confidence his sacrifice
made once for all upon the cross.

Bringing before you the bread of life and cup of salvation,
we proclaim his death and resurrection
until he comes in glory.

Praise to you, Lord Jesus:
Dying you destroyed our death,
rising you restored our life:
Lord Jesus, come in glory.

Lord of all life,
help us to work together for that day
when your kingdom comes
and justice and mercy will be seen in all the earth.

Look with favour on your people,
gather us in your loving arms
and bring us with [N and] all the saints
to feast at your table in heaven.

Through Christ, and with Christ, and in Christ,
in the unity of the Holy Spirit,
all honour and glory are yours, O loving Father,
for ever and ever.
Amen.

8 *Breaking of the Bread*

The president breaks the consecrated bread.

9 *Giving of Communion*

The president invites the congregation to receive Communion.

The president and people receive Communion.

Songs Christ above me (*The Source 2*)
Oh the mercy of God (*The Source 2*)
Friend of sinners (*The Source 2*)

Silence

Lord God,
the bright splendour whom the nations seek:
may we who with the wise men
have been drawn by your light

The music ends.

discern the glory of your presence in your Son,
the Word made flesh, Jesus Christ our Lord.

**Almighty God,
we thank you for feeding us
with the body and blood of your Son Jesus Christ.
Through him we offer you our souls and bodies
to be a living sacrifice.
Send us out in the power of your Spirit
to live and work to your praise and glory.
Amen.**

10 *Liturgy of the Word*

Reading 1

Silence

(Reading 2)

Silence

The reading(s) follow unannounced.

Short sermon
Less formal exposition. Drama, interviews, testimonies,
discussion or audio-visuals could be used within the
sermon or in between parts of the sermon.

Sermon linked to the overall theme if there
is one. Challenging and affirming, giving
practical help for discipleship. Contemporary
and relevant, linking with everyday life.

11 *Response and Worship*

During this time of sung worship people can be invited to
make a practical response. A large wooden cross could be
laid on the floor at the front of the church, a crown of
thorns could also be placed nearby – both symbols of the
King of Grace. A strip of coloured cloth could be placed
over every person's seat before the service. The congregation
would at this point in the service be invited to bring their
strip of cloth forward and whilst kneeling down as a sign
of worship, place the cloth on or near the cross. This
would be a sign of adoration for the newborn King, an
offering of a gift and a way of nailing their colours to the
mast by pinning their hopes on Jesus. People would be
free to stay kneeling at the front of church during this time
or free to remain seated refraining from taking part in the
response.

Worship leader to introduce this time of
sung worship and response. Guidance as to
how people might respond through the
worship needs to be given clearly.

Songs Jesus, what a beautiful name (*The Source*)
I bow my knee before your throne (*The Source*)
Wonderful Grace (*The Source 2*)

Songs linked using instrumental music.

Music ends.

12 *Open prayer*

(Guided prayers offered by the congregation either silently
or aloud)

Guidelines given regarding prayer topics through a prayer
leader or OHP headings. The congregation can be encouraged
to express prayers freely and as they feel comfortable (e.g.
out loud or silently). At a certain point the congregation

Music (live or recorded) could be played in
the background to the prayers. Projected
images or artwork could also be used
creatively. In some churches this form of
open prayer may lead to the sharing of
prophecies and other spiritual gifts.

could be invited to speak out prayers simultaneously. The congregation could also be split into groups for prayer, each group taking responsibility for a different topic.

- Prayer for the world
- Prayer for this country
- Prayer for the wider church
- Prayer for our own church
- Prayer for our community
- Prayer for those in need
- Prayer for the lost

13 *The Lord's Prayer*

As our Saviour taught us, so we pray

**Our Father in heaven,
hallowed be your name,
your kingdom come,
your will be done,
on earth as in heaven.
Give us today our daily bread.
Forgive us our sins
as we forgive those who sin against us.
Lead us not into temptation
but deliver us from evil.
For the kingdom, the power, and the glory are yours
now and for ever.
Amen.**

Stand
Song You are the sovereign 'I Am' (*The Source 2*)

14 *Affirmation of Faith*

Let us affirm our faith in Jesus Christ the Son of God.

**Though he was divine,
he did not cling to equality with God,
but made himself nothing.
Taking the form of a slave,
he was born in human likeness.
He humbled himself and was obedient to death,
even the death of the cross.
Therefore God has raised him on high,
and given him the name above every name:
that at the name of Jesus
every knee should bow,
and every voice proclaim that Jesus Christ is Lord,
to the glory of God the Father. Amen.**

Song Come, let us worship Jesus (vv 4 and 5) (*The Source*)

To conclude the time of prayer the Lord's Prayer is said.

As the Lord's Prayer is said a musical introduction for the song 'You are the sovereign "I Am"' starts.

The Affirmation of Faith follows on immediately after the song.

Lively but sensitive background music continues during the Affirmation of Faith.

Towards the end of the Affirmation of Faith the background music develops into a clear and bold introduction to the final song.

Music ends.

Before the Blessing offer the opportunity for prayer ministry following the Dismissal.

15 *The Blessing and Dismissal*

Christ the Son of God perfect in you
the image of his glory
and gladden your hearts
with the good news of his kingdom;
and the blessing of God almighty,
the Father, the Son, and the Holy Spirit,
be among you and remain with you always.
Amen.

Go in peace to love and serve the Lord.
In the name of Christ. Amen.

16 *Prayer Ministry Available*

Soft worship music could be played or
sung as people leave or as prayer continues.

Evening of Ash Wednesday
Service of the Word including the Laying on of Hands with Anointing and Holy Communion

Order of Service | Directions

1 Welcome and Introduction

Warm and inviting. Visitors and newcomers should be made particularly welcome.

If necessary, a clear outline of the service given. Where words for the worship may be found (e.g. service sheet, book, etc.)

Stand

2 Sung Worship
Song I will praise you (*Release*)

Move directly into sung worship.

3 Open Worship
(Open to God, open prayer or praise, reflecting, sharing gifts of the Spirit)

Sensitive instrumental music continues in the background. Open to the Holy Spirit. It may be appropriate to encourage the congregation to be free in their expression of worship at this point (e.g. to speak out prayer or to pray silently). It is important for the worship leader to direct worship sensitively at this point.

Silence

Sit if not already doing so.

4 Prayers of Penitence

The sacrifice of God is a broken spirit;
a broken and contrite heart God will not despise.
Let us come to the Lord, who is full of compassion,
and acknowledge our transgressions
in penitence and faith.

**Lord God,
we have sinned against you;
we have done evil in your sight.
We are sorry and repent.
Have mercy on us according to your love.
Wash away our wrongdoing
and cleanse us from our sin.
Renew a right spirit within us
and restore to us the joy of your salvation,
through Jesus Christ our Lord. Amen.**

Song Only by grace can we enter (*The Source*)

Musical introduction to 'Only by grace' begins unannounced immediately after the confession.

May the God of love and power
forgive *you* and free *you* from your sins,
heal and strengthen *you* by his Spirit,
and raise *you* to new life in Christ our Lord.
Amen.

Soft instrumental music continues in the background during the Absolution.

Music ends.

The day is almost over,
and the evening has come;
let us pray with one heart and mind.

Silence

5 The Collect

Almighty and everlasting God,
you hate nothing that you have made
and forgive the sins of all those who are penitent:
create and make in us new and contrite hearts
that we, worthily lamenting our sins
and acknowledging our wretchedness,
may receive from you, the God of all mercy,
perfect remission and forgiveness;
through Jesus Christ your Son our Lord,
who is alive and reigns with you,
in the unity of the Holy Spirit,
one God, now and for ever.
Amen.

The Collect follows unannounced.

6 The Word of God

Reading

Silence

The reading follows unannounced.

Short Sermon

Less formal exposition. Drama, interviews, testimonies,
discussion, stories, illustrations or audio-visuals could be
used within the talk or in between parts of the talk.

Silence

Space to reflect on the Sermon.

The Lord is my light and my salvation;
the Lord is the strength of my life.
The Lord is my light and my salvation;
the Lord is the strength of my life.
The light shines in the darkness
and the darkness has not overcome it.
The Lord is the strength of my life.
Glory to the Father, and to the Son
and to the Holy Spirit.
The Lord is my light and my salvation
the Lord is the strength of my life.

Musical introduction to 'To you, O Lord'
begins on the words 'The Lord is my light
and my salvation'.

Song To you, O Lord, I lift up my soul (*The Source*)

7 Affirmation of Faith

Let us declare our faith in God:

We believe in God the Father,
from whom every family
in heaven and on earth is named.

We believe in God the Son,
who lives in our hearts through faith,
and fills us with his love.

Instrumental music continues in the
background to the Affirmation of Faith.

**We believe in God the Holy Spirit,
who strengthens us
with power from on high.**

**We believe in one God;
Father, Son and Holy Spirit. Amen.**

8   *Intercessions*

The music ends and the prayers follow unannounced.

God the Father, your will for all people
is health and salvation.
We praise and bless you, Lord.

God the Son, you came that we might have life,
and might have it more abundantly.
We praise and bless you, Lord.

God the Holy Spirit, you make our bodies
the temple of your presence.
We praise and bless you, Lord.

Silence

Holy Trinity, one God, in you we live and move
and have our being.
We praise and bless you, Lord.

Lord, grant your healing grace to all who are sick,
injured or disabled,
that they may be made whole.
Hear us, Lord of life.

Grant to all who are lonely, anxious or depressed
a knowledge of your will
and an awareness of your presence.
Hear us, Lord of life.

Silence

Grant to all who minister to those who are suffering
wisdom and skill, sympathy and patience.
Hear us, Lord of life.

Mend broken relationships, and restore to those in distress
soundness of mind and serenity of spirit.
Hear us, Lord of life.

Sustain and support those who seek your guidance
and lift up all who are brought low
by the trials of this life.
Hear us, Lord of life.

Grant to the dying peace and a holy death,
and uphold by the grace and consolation
of your Holy Spirit
Those who are bereaved.
Hear us, Lord of life.

Restore to wholeness whatever is broken by human sin,
in our lives, in our nation, and in the world.
Hear us, Lord of life.

Silence

You are the Lord who does mighty wonders.
You have declared your power among the peoples.

With you, Lord, is the well of life.
and in your light do we see light.

Hear us, Lord of life,
heal us, and make us whole.

Silence

O Lord our God,
accept the fervent prayers of your people;
in the multitude of your mercies look with compassion
upon us and all who turn to you for help;
for you are gracious, O lover of souls,
and to you we give glory, Father, Son, and Holy Spirit,
now and for ever.
Amen.

9 *Liturgy Introduction to the Laying on of Hands with Anointing*

Praise God who made heaven and earth,
who keeps his promise for ever.

Let us give thanks to the Lord our God,
who is worthy of all thanksgiving and praise.

Blessed are you, Sovereign God, gentle and merciful,
creator of heaven and earth.
Your Word brought light out of darkness,
and daily your Spirit renews the face of the earth.

Your anointed Son brought healing
to those in weakness and distress.
He broke the power of evil
and set us free from sin and death
that we might praise your name for ever.

By the power of your Spirit may your blessing rest
on those who are anointed with this oil in your name;
may they be made whole in body, mind and spirit,
restored in your image, renewed in your love,
and serve you as sons and daughters in your kingdom.

Through your anointed Son, Jesus Christ, our Lord,
to whom with you and the Holy Spirit
we lift our voices of thanks and praise:

**Blessed be God, our strength and our salvation,
now and for ever. Amen.**

10 *Extended Time of Sung Worship and the Laying on of Hands with Anointing*

A time of sung worship to facilitate this response. The worship leader should direct clearly and sensitively at this point. Openness to gifts of the Spirit could be encouraged at the beginning or end of this part of the service. Prophecies or Words of Knowledge could be shared. People could remain in their seats to worship or pray quietly and those seeking the Laying on of Hands could be invited to come forward.

The Laying on of Hands is administered using suitable words.

As the Anointing is administered the minister says:

N, I anoint you in the name of God who gives you life.
Receive Christ's forgiveness, his healing and his love.

May the Father of our Lord Jesus Christ
grant you the riches of his grace,
his wholeness and his peace.
Amen.

Songs/Hymns during the Laying on of Hands with Anointing

Rock of ages (New version – *The Source 2*)
Breathe on me Breath of God (*The Source*)
Oh kneel me down again (*The Source 2*)
Jesus you are my King (*Release*)

Songs linked with instrumental music. Sensitive background music could continue during any open worship.

11 *Prayer to Conclude Time of Laying on of Hands with Anointing*

The almighty Lord,
who is a strong tower for all who put their trust in him,
whom all things in heaven, on earth and under the earth obey,
be now and evermore your defence.
May you believe and trust that the only name under heaven
given for health and salvation
is the name of our Lord Jesus Christ.
Amen.

12 *The Peace*

Since we are justified by faith,
we have peace with God through our Lord Jesus Christ,
who has given us access to his grace.

The peace of the Lord be always with you
and also with you.

Let us offer one another a sign of peace.

All may exchange a sign of peace.

The table is prepared during the Peace.

13 *Eucharistic Prayer (E)*

The Lord be with you
and also with you.

Lift up your hearts.
We lift them to the Lord.

Let us give thanks to the Lord our God.
It is right to give thanks and praise.

It is indeed right and good
to give you thanks and praise,
almighty God and everlasting Father,
through Jesus Christ your Son.
For in these forty days
you lead us into the desert of repentance
that through a pilgrimage of prayer and discipline
we may grow in grace
and learn to be your people once again.

The Eucharistic Prayer follows on immediately after the Peace

Through fasting, prayer and acts of service
you bring us back to your generous heart.
Through study of your holy word
you open our eyes to your presence in the world
and free our hands to welcome others
into the radiant splendour of your love.
As we prepare to celebrate the Easter feast
with joyful hearts and minds
we bless you for your mercy
and join with saints and angels
for ever praising you and *saying*:

Holy, holy, holy Lord,
God of power and might,
heaven and earth are full of your glory.
Hosanna in the highest.
[Blessed is he who comes in the name of the Lord.
Hosanna in the highest.]

We praise and bless you, loving Father,
through Jesus Christ, our Lord;
and as we obey his command,
send your Holy Spirit,
that broken bread and wine outpoured
may be for us the body and blood of your dear Son.

On the night before he died
he had supper with his friends
and, taking bread, he praised you.
He broke the bread, gave it to them and said:
Take, eat; this is my body which is given for you;
do this in remembrance of me.

When supper was ended he took the cup of wine.
Again he praised you, gave it to them and said:
Drink this, all of you;
this is my blood of the new covenant,
which is shed for you and for many
for the forgiveness of sins.
Do this, as often as you drink it, in remembrance of me.

So, Father, we remember all that Jesus did,
in him we plead with confidence his sacrifice
made once for all upon the cross.

Bringing before you the bread of life and cup of salvation,
we proclaim his death and resurrection
until he comes in glory.

Jesus Christ is Lord:
Lord, by your cross and resurrection
you have set us free.
You are the Saviour of the world.

Lord of all life,
help us to work together for that day
when your kingdom comes
and justice and mercy will be seen in all the earth.

Look with favour on your people,
gather us in your loving arms
and bring us with [N and] all the saints
to feast at your table in heaven.

Through Christ, and with Christ, and in Christ,
in the unity of the Holy Spirit,
all honour and glory are yours, O loving Father,
for ever and ever.
Amen.

14 *Breaking of the Bread*

The president breaks the consecrated bread.

15 *Giving of Communion*

The president invites the congregation to receive Communion.

The president and the people receive Communion.

(If space allows for the number of people present, the congregation could come to the table together and the bread and wine could be passed around the whole group.)

During Communion
Silence/recorded music (classical or contemporary)/
worship songs led by the music group or worship band.

Song Name above all names (*The Source 2*)

After Communion the final song is announced.

16 *Blessing*

Christ give you grace to grow in holiness,
to deny yourselves, take up your cross, and follow him;
and the blessing of God almighty,
the Father, the Son, and the Holy Spirit,
be among you and remain with you always.
Amen.

Before the Blessing offer the opportunity for prayer ministry before people leave.

17 *Prayer Ministry Available*

Gentle worship songs could be sung as people leave or as prayer continues.

First Sunday of Lent
Service of the Word

Order of Service

1 **Welcome and Introduction**

Remain seated

2 **Opening Prayer**

(The worship leader opens the worship in prayer)

3 **Sentence of Scripture**

. . . Christ died for sins once for all, the righteous for the unrighteous, to bring you to God. (1 Peter 3:18)

Silence

4 **Confession**

Father eternal, giver of light and grace,
we have sinned against you
and against our neighbour,
in what we have thought,
in what we have said and done,
through ignorance, through weakness,
through our own deliberate fault.
We have wounded your love
and marred your image in us.
We are sorry and ashamed
and repent of all our sins.
For the sake of your Son Jesus Christ,
who died for us,
forgive us all that is past
and lead us out from darkness
to walk as children of light.
Amen.

5 **Absolution**

Almighty God, our heavenly Father,
who in his great mercy
has promised forgiveness of sins
to all those who with heartfelt repentance
and true faith
turn to him:
have mercy on *you*,
pardon and deliver *you* from all *your* sins,
confirm and strengthen *you* in all goodness,
and bring *you* to everlasting life,
through Jesus Christ our Lord.
Amen.

Directions

Warm and inviting. Visitors and newcomers should be made particularly welcome.

If necessary, a clear outline of the service given. Where words for the worship may be found (e.g. service sheet, book, etc.)

Move directly into the opening prayer

An image of Christ on the cross could be projected onto a screen whilst the sentence of scripture is read and during the short period of silence.

6 *Collect*

> Almighty God,
> whose Son Jesus Christ fasted forty days in the wilderness,
> and was tempted as we are, yet without sin:
> give us grace to discipline ourselves
> in obedience to your Spirit;
> and, as you know our weakness,
> so may we know your power to save;
> through Jesus Christ your Son our Lord,
> who is alive and reigns with you,
> in the unity of the Holy Spirit,
> one God, now and for ever.
> **Amen.**

Stand

7 *Extended Time of Sung Worship*

Songs/Hymns

Praise to the holiest in the height
(*Complete Anglican Hymns Old and New*)
Come let us worship Jesus (*The Source*)
Saviour I will sing to you (*Release*)
All I want is to know you, Jesus (*The Source 2*)

8 *Open Worship*

(Open to God, open prayer or praise, reflecting, sharing
gifts of the Spirit)

Silence

9 *The Word*

Reading

Silence

Talk

Less formal exposition. Drama, interviews, testimonies,
discussion, stories, illustrations or audio-visuals could be
used within the talk or in between parts of the talk.

Silence

10 *Response*

Intercessory Worship

Sung worship providing the framework for, or leading
into, open prayer (prayers offered by the congregation
either silently or aloud).

A song or part of one could be used as a refrain during
the intercessions. It could be used to conclude each
section of prayer. Alternatively, a collection of songs could
lead into the intercessions. Prayers could be directed and
guided by headings projected onto a screen. Alternatively,
a prayer leader could say spontaneous or written prayers

The Collect follows unannounced.

Extended Time of Sung Worship is
announced.

Songs and hymns linked with instrumental
music.

Sensitive instrumental music continues in
the background. Open to the Holy Spirit.
It may be appropriate to encourage the
congregation to be free in their expression
of worship at this point (e.g. to speak out
prayer or to pray silently). It is important
for the worship leader to direct worship
sensitively at this point.

The reading follows the silence
unannounced.

The Bible reference is given.

Talk linked to the overall theme if there
is one. Challenging and affirming, giving
practical help for discipleship. Contemporary
and relevant, linking with everyday life.

Silence used to reflect on the Talk.

whilst leaving space for open prayer. In some churches this form of open prayer may lead to the sharing of prophecies and other spiritual gifts. Some gifted musicians or members of the congregation may be able to sing prayers or prophecies. This could be facilitated during this section of worship. Projected images, artwork, dance and signing could also be used creatively within this section of the service.

Suggested songs to be used
All who are thirsty (*The Source 2*)
I lift my eyes up to the mountains (*The Source*)
This is your house (*The Source 2*)

or

Prayer Ministry
An extended time of sung worship could be used to facilitate prayer ministry. The congregation would be invited to respond by coming forward to receive prayer with the laying on of hands. Guidance could be given as to what people might want to receive prayer for. Alternatively people could respond privately by remaining in their seats and participating in the worship. Intercessory worship could follow prayer ministry.

Suggested songs to be used
I lift my eyes up to the mountains (*The Source*)
As the deer (Lewis version, *The Source*)
Jesus, be the centre (*The Source 2*)

11 *Conclusion*

As the worship is drawn to a close prayer ministry may continue. It is important, however, that the service has a clear and satisfactory ending. A final prayer could be said by the worship leader, or an appropriate concluding prayer could be used from *Common Worship*.

Song The Grace (*The Source 2*)

12 *Prayer Ministry Available*

Background music could be played during times of open prayer.

Songs linked using extended times of instrumental music. Music could be played in the background to any instructions or guidance being given.

Soft background music could continue during the concluding prayer.

Before the Grace offer the opportunity for prayer ministry.

Soft worship music could continue as people leave or as prayer continues.

Palm Sunday
Service of the Word

Order of Service

1 Welcome and Introduction

Stand

2 Opening Prayer

(The worship/service leader opens the worship in prayer)

3 Sentence of Scripture

Give thanks to the Lord, for he is good; his love endures forever. (Psalm 118:1)

4 Extended Time of Sung Worship

Songs/Hymns

Great is he who's the King of kings (*The Source 2*)
All glory, laud and honour
(*Complete Anglican Hymns Old & New*)
I trust in you, my faithful Lord (*The Source 2*)

5 Open Worship

(Open to God, open prayer or praise, reflecting, sharing gifts of the Spirit)

Silence

Sit if not doing so already.

6 Confession

God shows his love for us
in that, while we were still sinners, Christ died for us.
Let us then show our love for him
by confessing our sins in penitence and faith.

**Lord God,
we have sinned against you;
we have done evil in your sight.
We are sorry and repent.
Have mercy on us according to your love.
Wash away our wrongdoing
and cleanse us from our sin.
Renew a right spirit within us
and restore to us the joy of your salvation,
through Jesus Christ our Lord. Amen.**

Directions

Warm and inviting. Visitors and newcomers should be made particularly welcome.

If necessary, a clear outline of the service could be given. Where words for the worship may be found (e.g. service sheet, book, etc.).

Move directly into the opening prayer.

Musical introduction to the first song begins immediately after the sentence of scripture.

Songs and hymns linked with instrumental music.

Sensitive instrumental music continues in the background. Open to the Holy Spirit. It may be appropriate to encourage the congregation to be free in their expression of worship at this point (e.g. to speak out prayer or to pray silently). It is important for the worship leader to direct worship sensitively at this point.

Background music may continue for a time whilst the people remain silent. At an appropriate moment the music ends.

May the Father of all mercies
cleanse *you* from *your* sins,
and restore *you* in his image
to the praise and glory of his name,
through Jesus Christ our Lord.
Amen.

Silence

7 *Collect*

Almighty and everlasting God,
who in your tender love towards the human race
sent your Son our Saviour Jesus Christ
to take upon him our flesh
and to suffer death upon the cross:
grant that we may follow the example
of his patience and humility,
and also be made partakers of his resurrection;
through Jesus Christ your Son our Lord.
Amen.

> As the service leader says the Collect the musical introduction to the next song begins softly and builds in volume.

Song Alleluia, Alleluia (*The Source 2*)

> End the song by singing the final chorus unaccompanied.

8 *The Word*
Reading 1

Silence

> The reading follows unannounced.

(Reading 2)

Silence

> If there is one, the second reading follows the silence unannounced.

Talk
Less formal exposition. Drama, interviews, testimonies, discussion, stories, illustrations or audio-visuals could be used within the talk or in between parts of the talk.

> Talk linked to the overall theme if there is one. Challenging and affirming, giving practical help for discipleship. Contemporary and relevant, linking with everyday life.

9 *Response*
Period of silence

> Silence used for reflection or prayer.

Liquid Intercessions (approx. 15 min)
A number of different forms of prayer are provided in allocated parts of the church. The congregation is free to take part in the prayer options and to move between them as and when they choose during the allotted time. You may of course come up with your own forms of creative prayer options to use but here are some suggestions:

> Clear instructions are needed regarding how people are to pray.

Intercessory worship
Provided in the main part of church. Sung worship providing the framework for, or leading into, open prayer (prayers offered by the congregation either silently or aloud). A song or part of one could be used as a refrain during the intercessions. It could be used to conclude each section of prayer. Alternatively, a collection of songs could lead into the intercessions. Prayers could be directed and guided by

headings projected onto a screen. Alternatively, a prayer leader could say spoken or written prayers whilst leaving space for open prayer. In some churches this form of open prayer may lead to the sharing of prophecies and other spiritual gifts. Some gifted musicians or members of the congregation may be able to sing prayers or prophecies. This could be facilitated during this section of worship. Projected images, artwork, dance and signing could also be used creatively within this section of the service.

Prayer in groups
A part of the church could be given over to the option of praying with others.

Visual prayer
Images (e.g. news video footage or photos), newspaper headlines, sentences of scripture and prayer headings are projected onto the screen whilst appropriate background music is played (live or from a CD). People are able to pray silently as prompted by what they see or read. This option could be used as part of intercessory worship.

Private prayer
The option for people to remain seated where they are and to pray privately. Or a space provided for reflective prayer, e.g. candles, cushions and soft music.

10 **The Lord's Prayer**

As our Saviour taught us, so we pray

Our Father in heaven,
hallowed be your name,
your kingdom come,
your will be done,
on earth as in heaven.
Give us today our daily bread.
Forgive us our sins
as we forgive those who sin against us.
Lead us not into temptation
but deliver us from evil.
For the kingdom, the power, and the glory are yours
now and for ever. Amen.

Stand

11 **Time of Sung Worship**

Songs/Hymns
My song is love unknown
(*Complete Anglican Hymns Old & New*)
Say the name of love (*The Source 2*)

12 **Affirmation of Faith**

Let us affirm our faith in Jesus Christ the Son of God.

Though he was divine,
he did not cling to equality with God,
but made himself nothing.

Towards the end of the intercessions draw people back to their places. The Lord's Prayer is said to conclude the intercessions.

Immediately after the Lord's Prayer the musical introduction to the next hymn begins.

Hymn and song linked through instrumental music.

Song ends boldly.

Taking the form of a slave,
he was born in human likeness.
He humbled himself
and was obedient to death,
even the death of the cross.
Therefore God has raised him on high,
and given him the name above every name:
that at the name of Jesus
every knee should bow,
and every voice proclaim that Jesus Christ is Lord,
to the glory of God the Father. Amen.

13 *Concluding Prayer*

A final prayer could be said by the service/worship leader, or an appropriate concluding prayer could be used from *Common Worship* or *Patterns for Worship*.

14 *Blessing*

Christ crucified draw you to himself,
to find in him a sure ground for faith,
a firm support for hope,
and the assurance of sins forgiven;
and the blessing of God almighty,
the Father, the Son, and the Holy Spirit,
be among you and remain with you always.
Amen.

Go in peace to love and serve the Lord.
In the name of Christ. Amen.

15 *Prayer Ministry Available*

Before the Blessing and Dismissal offer the opportunity for prayer ministry.

Soft worship music could continue as people leave or as prayer continues.

Good Friday
Meditations on the Word

This service outline provides a simple framework. Further audio-visual, drama or dance ideas could be added where appropriate.

Order of Service

Silence as people enter

1 **Welcome and Introduction**

2 **Opening Prayer**

(The worship/service leader opens the worship in prayer)

3 **First Reading**

John 18:1-27

Silence

Remain seated
Song Come, ye sinners, poor and needy (*The Source 2*)

4 **Confession**

Lord Jesus Christ,
we confess we have failed you as did your first disciples.
We ask for your mercy and your help.

Our selfishness betrays you:
Lord, forgive us.
Christ have mercy.

We fail to share the pain of your suffering:
Lord, forgive us.
Christ have mercy.

We run away from those who abuse you:
Lord, forgive us.
Christ have mercy.

We are afraid of being known to belong to you:
Lord, forgive us.
Christ have mercy.

Time given for personal prayer and reflection.

May the Father of all mercies
cleanse *you* from *your* sins,
and restore *you* in his image
to the praise and glory of his name,
through Jesus Christ our Lord.
Amen.

Directions

Warm and inviting. Visitors and newcomers should be made particularly welcome.

If necessary, a clear outline of the service given. Where words for the worship may be found (e.g. service sheet, book, etc.)

Move directly into the opening prayer.

The first reading follows the prayer unannounced.

For meditation on the reading.

Musical introduction to the first song begins after a few minutes of silence.

Sensitive instrumental music continues in the background to the Confession.

Background music continues whilst the people remain silent. After a few minutes the music ends.

5 *Second Reading*

John 18:28-40

Silence

Stand
Song Name above all names (*The Source 2*)

Let us affirm our faith in Jesus Christ the Son of God.

**Though he was divine,
he did not cling to equality with God,
but made himself nothing.
Taking the form of a slave,
he was born in human likeness.
He humbled himself
and was obedient to death,
even the death of the cross.
Therefore God has raised him on high,
and given him the name above every name:
that at the name of Jesus
every knee should bow,
and every voice proclaim that Jesus Christ is Lord,
to the glory of God the Father. Amen.**

Sit
Time given for personal prayer and reflection.

6 *Third Reading*

John 19:1-16a

Silence

Remain seated
Hymn My song is love unknown (*The Source 2*)

Time given for personal prayer and reflection.

7 *Fourth Reading*

John 19:16b-27

Silence

Intercessory worship
Sung worship providing the framework for, or leading into, open prayer (prayers offered by the congregation either silently or aloud).

A song or part of one could be used as a refrain during the intercessions. It could be used to conclude each section of prayer. Alternatively, a collection of songs could lead into the intercessions. Prayers could be directed and guided by headings projected onto a screen. Alternatively, a prayer leader could say spoken or written prayers whilst leaving space for open prayer. In some churches this form

The second reading follows the absolution unannounced.

For meditation on the reading.

Musical introduction to the song begins after a few minutes of silence.

The Affirmation of Faith follows immediately after the song.

After a few minutes of silence the third reading follows unannounced.

For meditation on the reading.

Musical introduction to the hymn begins after a few minutes of silence.

Background music continues whilst the people remain silent. After several minutes the music ends.

After a few minutes of silence the fourth reading follows unannounced.

For meditation on the reading.

of open prayer may lead to the sharing of prophecies and other spiritual gifts. Some gifted musicians or members of the congregation may be able to sing prayers or prophecies. This could be facilitated during this section of worship. Projected images, artwork, dance and signing could also be used creatively within this section of the service.

Songs/Hymns On the blood-stained ground (*The Source 2*)
Here is love (*The Source*)
Filled with compassion (*The Source*)

An extended musical introduction to the first song could be played whilst people continue to meditate and reflect.

Songs and hymns linked with instrumental music. Background music continues in between songs to facilitate open worship and prayer.

8 *Fifth Reading*

John 19:28-42

Silence

Hymn It is a thing most wonderful (*The Source 2*)

Fifth reading follows immediately after the time of intercessory worship.

For meditation on the reading.

Musical introduction to the hymn begins after a few minutes of silence.

Before the Blessing and Dismissal offer the opportunity for prayer ministry.

9 *Blessing*

The peace of God,
which passes all understanding,
keep your hearts and minds
in the knowledge and love of God,
and of his Son Jesus Christ our Lord;
and the blessing of God almighty,
the Father, the Son, and the Holy Spirit,
be among you and remain with you always.
Amen.

Go in peace to love and serve the Lord.
In the name of Christ. Amen.

10 *Prayer Ministry Available*

Soft worship music could continue as people leave or as prayer continues.

Easter Day
Service of Holy Communion

Order of Service

1 The Gathering

(People enter as music is played, e.g. music group or band, organ, recorded music – contemporary or classical)

2 The Greeting

The Lord be with you
and also with you.

Alleluia. Christ is risen.
He is risen indeed. Alleluia.

3 Welcome and Notices

4 Introduction

Stand

5 Prayer of Preparation

**Almighty God,
to whom all hearts are open,
all desires known,
and from whom no secrets are hidden:
cleanse the thoughts of our hearts
by the inspiration of your Holy Spirit,
that we may perfectly love you,
and worthily magnify your holy name;
through Christ our Lord.
Amen.**

6 Extended Time of Sung Worship

Song Your love is amazing (*The Source 2*)
Hymn Thine be the glory (*The Source*)
Song Saviour, I will sing to you (*Release*)

7 Open Worship

(Open to God, open prayer or praise, reflecting, sharing gifts of the Spirit)

Silence

Sit if not already doing so.

Directions

Warm and inviting. Visitors and newcomers should be made particularly welcome.

A clear verbal outline of the service could be given.

SHORT PAUSE

Music introduction to 'Your love is amazing' begins on the words 'worthily magnify'.

After the prayer move directly into sung praise and worship.

Sensitive instrumental music continues in the background. Open to the Holy Spirit. It may be appropriate to encourage the congregation to be free in their expression of worship at this point (e.g. to speak out prayer or to pray silently). It is important for the worship leader to direct worship sensitively at this point.

8 *Confession*

Jesus Christ, risen Master and triumphant Lord,
we come to you in sorrow for our sins,
and confess to you our weakness and unbelief.

We have lived by our own strength,
and not by the power of your resurrection.
In your mercy, forgive us.
Lord, hear us and help us.

We have lived by the light of our own eyes,
as faithless and not believing.
In your mercy, forgive us.
Lord, hear us and help us.

We have lived for this world alone,
and doubted our home in heaven.
In your mercy, forgive us.
Lord, hear us and help us.

May the God of love and power
forgive *you* and free *you* from *your* sins,
heal and strengthen *you* by his Spirit,
and raise *you* to new life in Christ our Lord.
Amen.

Hymn Thine be the glory (chorus)

9 *Collect*

Silence

Lord of all life and power,
who through the mighty resurrection of your Son
overcame the old order of sin and death
to make all things new in him:
grant that we, being dead to sin
and alive to you in Jesus Christ,
may reign with him in glory;
to whom with you and the Holy Spirit
be praise and honour, glory and might,
now and in all eternity.
Amen.

10 *The Liturgy of the Word*

Reading 1

Short time of silence

Gospel Reading
Alleluia, alleluia.
I am the first and the last, says the Lord,
and the living one;
I was dead, and behold I am alive for evermore.
Alleluia.

Music introduction to 'Thine be the glory'
begins and leads into the singing of the
hymn following the Absolution.

Music ends.

The Collect follows unannounced.

The readings follow unannounced.

When the Gospel is announced the reader says

Hear the Gospel of our Lord Jesus Christ according to *N*.
Glory to you, O Lord.

Following the gospel reading

This is the Gospel of the Lord.
Praise to you, O Christ.

Short time of silence

Sermon

Less formal exposition. Drama, interviews, testimonies, discussion, stories, illustrations or audio-visuals could be used within the sermon or in between parts of the sermon.

Silence

11 *Intercessory Worship*

Sung worship providing the framework for, or leading into, open prayer (prayers offered by the congregation either silently or aloud).

After the singing of 'This is your house' space could be left for open prayer along the themes given in the headings below – prayer could be directed by projecting the headings onto a screen. Alternatively, a prayer leader could guide through spoken or written prayers leaving space for open prayer. After each section of prayer the chorus of 'This is your house' could be repeated. In some churches this form of open prayer may lead to the sharing of prophecies and other spiritual gifts. Some gifted musicians or members of the congregation may be able to sing prayers or prophecies. Projected images, artwork, dance and signing could also be used creatively within this section of the service.

Songs We bow down (*The Source 2*)
　　　This is your house (*The Source 2*)

- Prayer for the world
- Prayer for this country
- **Song** This is your house (chorus)
- Prayer for the wider church
- Prayer for our own church
- **Song** This is your house (chorus)
- Prayer for our community
- Prayer for those in need
- **Song** This is your house (chorus)
- Prayer for the lost
- **Song** This is your house (chorus)

Sermon linked to the overall theme if there is one. Challenging and affirming, giving practical help for discipleship. Contemporary and relevant, linking with everyday life.

Silence used to reflect on the Sermon.

Songs linked with instrumental music.

Sensitive background music continues.

After each section of prayer a musical introduction leads into the singing of the chorus from 'This is your house'.

Music ends.

Stand

12 The Nicene Creed

> We believe in one God,
> the Father, the Almighty,
> maker of heaven and earth,
> of all that is,
> seen and unseen.
>
> We believe in one Lord, Jesus Christ,
> the only Son of God,
> eternally begotten of the Father,
> God from God, Light from Light,
> true God from true God,
> begotten, not made,
> of one Being with the Father;
> through him all things were made.
> For us and for our salvation
> he came down from heaven,
> was incarnate from the Holy Spirit
> and the Virgin Mary
> and was made man.
> For our sake he was crucified under Pontius Pilate;
> he suffered death and was buried.
> On the third day he rose again
> in accordance with the Scriptures;
> he ascended into heaven
> and is seated at the right hand of the Father.
> He will come again in glory
> to judge the living and the dead,
> and his kingdom will have no end.
>
> We believe in the Holy Spirit,
> the Lord, the giver of life,
> who proceeds from the Father and the Son,
> who with the Father and the Son
> is worshipped and glorified,
> who has spoken through the prophets.
> We believe in one holy catholic and apostolic Church.
> We acknowledge one baptism
> for the forgiveness of sins.
> We look for the resurrection of the dead,
> and the life of the world to come.
> Amen.

13 The Peace

> The risen Christ came and stood among his disciples
> and said, 'Peace be with you.'
> Then were they glad when they saw the Lord. Alleluia.
>
> The peace of the Lord be always with you
> **and also with you.**
>
> Let us offer one another a sign of peace.

All may exchange a sign of peace.

Hymn Crown him with many crowns (vv 1-4) (*The Source*)

At an appropriate point following the Peace the music introduction to the hymn 'Crown him with many crowns' begins.

14 *Eucharistic Prayer (A)*

The Lord be with you
and also with you.

Lift up your hearts.
We lift them to the Lord.

Let us give thanks to the Lord our God.
It is right to give thanks and praise.

It is indeed right, our duty and our joy,
always and everywhere to give you thanks,
almighty and eternal Father,
and in these days of Easter
to celebrate with joyful hearts
the memory of your wonderful works.
For by the mystery of his passion
Jesus Christ, your risen Son,
has conquered the powers of death and hell
and restored in men and women the image of your glory.
He has placed them once more in paradise
and opened to them the gate of life eternal.
And so, in the joy of this Passover,
earth and heaven resound with gladness,
while angels and archangels and the powers of all creation
sing for ever the hymn of your glory:

Holy, holy, holy Lord,
God of power and might,
heaven and earth are full of your glory.
Hosanna in the highest.
[Blessed is he who comes in the name of the Lord.
Hosanna in the highest.]

Accept our praises, heavenly Father,
through your Son our Saviour Jesus Christ,
and as we follow his example and obey his command,
grant that by the power of your Holy Spirit
these gifts of bread and wine
may be to us his body and his blood;

who, in the same night that he was betrayed,
took bread and gave you thanks;
he broke it and gave it to his disciples, saying:
Take, eat; this is my body which is given for you;
do this in remembrance of me.

In the same way, after supper
he took the cup and gave you thanks;
he gave it to them, saying:
Drink this, all of you;
this is my blood of the new covenant,
which is shed for you and for many
for the forgiveness of sins.
Do this, as often as you drink it,
in remembrance of me.

Therefore, heavenly Father,
we remember his offering of himself
made once for all upon the cross;
we proclaim his mighty resurrection
and glorious ascension;

Instrumental of 'Crown him with many crowns' continues sensitively in background during Eucharistic Prayer.

we look for the coming of your kingdom,
and with this bread and this cup
we make the memorial of Christ your Son our Lord.

Christ has died:
Christ is risen:
Christ will come again.

Accept through him, our great high priest,
this our sacrifice of thanks and praise,
and as we eat and drink these holy gifts
in the presence of your divine majesty,
renew us by your Spirit,
inspire us with your love
and unite us in the body of your Son,
Jesus Christ our Lord.

Through him, and with him, and in him,
in the unity of the Holy Spirit,
with all who stand before you in earth and heaven,
we worship you, Father almighty,
in songs of everlasting praise:

Blessing and honour and glory and power
be yours for ever and ever.
Amen.

Hymn Crown him with many crowns (v 5) (*The Source*)

15 *The Lord's Prayer*

As our Saviour taught us, so we pray
Our Father in heaven,
hallowed be your name,
your kingdom come,
your will be done,
on earth as in heaven.
Give us today our daily bread.
Forgive us our sins
as we forgive those who sin against us.
Lead us not into temptation
but deliver us from evil.
For the kingdom, the power, and the glory are yours
now and for ever.
Amen.

16 *Breaking of the Bread*

The president breaks the consecrated bread.
We break this bread
to share in the body of Christ.
Though we are many, we are one body,
because we all share in one bread.

17 *Giving of Communion*

The president says the invitation to Communion
Alleluia. Christ our passover is sacrificed for us.
Therefore let us keep the feast. Alleluia.

The background music leads into a clear
and bold introduction to the final verse of
'Crown him with many crowns'.

Music ends.

Most merciful Lord,
your love compels us to come in.
Our hands were unclean,
our hearts were unprepared;
we were not fit
even to eat the crumbs from under your table.
But you, Lord, are the God of our salvation,
and share your bread with sinners.
So cleanse and feed us
with the precious body and blood of your Son,
that he may live in us and we in him;
and that we, with the whole company of Christ,
may sit and eat in your kingdom.
Amen.

The president and people receive Communion.

Songs On the blood-stained ground (*The Source 2*)
I will offer up my life (*The Source*)
Name above all names (*The Source 2*)

Songs linked with instrumental music.

Prayer ministry could be made available at an appropriate place within the church during Communion.

Music ends.

18 *Prayer after Communion*

Silence

God of Life,
who for our redemption gave your only-begotten Son
to the death of the cross,
and by his glorious resurrection
have delivered us from the power of our enemy:
grant us so to die daily to sin,
that we may evermore live with him
in the joy of his risen life;
through Jesus Christ our Lord.

**Father of all,
we give you thanks and praise,
that when we were still far off
you met us in your Son and brought us home.
Dying and living, he declared your love,
gave us grace, and opened the gate of glory.
May we who share Christ's body live his risen life;
we who drink his cup bring life to others;
we whom the Spirit lights give light to the world.
Keep us firm in the hope you have set before us,
so we and all your children shall be free,
and the whole earth live to praise your name;
through Christ our Lord.
Amen.**

Following the prayer the song 'Thank you, thank you for the blood' is announced.

Songs Thank you, thank you for the blood
(*world wide worship 2*)
Jesus Christ is risen today (*The Source*)

Before the Blessing and Dismissal offer the opportunity for prayer ministry.

19 *The Blessing and Dismissal*

    The God of peace,
    who brought again from the dead our Lord Jesus,
    that great shepherd of the sheep,
    through the blood of the eternal covenant,
    make you perfect in every good work to do his will,
    working in you that which is well-pleasing in his sight;
    and the blessing of God almighty,
    the Father, the Son, and the Holy Spirit,
    be among you and remain with you always.
    Amen.

    Go in the peace of Christ. Alleluia, Alleluia.
    Thanks be to God. Alleluia, Alleluia.

    Song The Grace (*The Source 2*)

20 *Prayer Ministry Available*

The Grace is sung to each other.

Soft worship music could be played or sung as people leave or as prayer continues.

Trinity Sunday
Service of the Word with Holy Communion

Order of Service	Directions

Order of Service

1 Welcome and Notices

2 Introduction

Stand

3 Extended Time of Sung Worship

Songs/Hymns
To the King eternal (*The Source 2*)
Immortal, invisible (*The Bridge*)
You are beautiful beyond description (*The Source*)

4 Open Worship

(Open to God, open prayer or praise, reflecting, sharing gifts of the Spirit, sharing testimony)

Silence

Sit if not doing so already.

5 Confession

Holy, holy, holy is the Lord Almighty;
the whole earth is full of his glory.
As we too look upon the Lord we cry with Isaiah
'Woe to me! I am ruined
for I am a person of unclean lips
and I live among a people of unclean lips
and my eyes have seen the King,
the Lord almighty.'
Spirit of God we need you to cleanse us,
to make clean our lips and sweep away our sin.
To breath new life in us.
We lift our eyes to you, Lord,
and confess the burden of our hearts.

**O King enthroned on high,
filling the earth with your glory:
holy is your name,
Lord God almighty.
In our sinfulness we cry to you
to take our guilt away,
and to cleanse our lips to speak your word,
through Jesus Christ our Lord.
Amen.**

Directions

Warm and inviting. Visitors and newcomers should be made particularly welcome.

A clear verbal outline of the service could be given.

Songs and hymns linked using instrumental music.

Sensitive instrumental music continues in the background. Open to the Holy Spirit. It may be appropriate to encourage the congregation to be free to worship as they feel led at this point (e.g. to speak out prayer/praise or to pray silently). It is important for the worship leader to direct worship sensitively at this point.

Music ends.

May the Father of all mercies
cleanse *us* from *our* sins,
and restore *us* in his image
to the praise and glory of his name,
through Jesus Christ our Lord.
Amen.

Song Just let me say (*The Source 2*)

Silence

6 *Collect*

Almighty and everlasting God,
you have given us your servants grace,
by the confession of a true faith,
to acknowledge the glory of the eternal Trinity
and in the power of the divine majesty
to worship the Unity:
keep us steadfast in this faith,
that we may evermore be defended from all adversities;
through Jesus Christ your Son our Lord,
who is alive and reigns with you,
in the unity of the Holy Spirit,
one God, now and for ever.

7 *Liturgy of the Word*

Reading 1

Silence

(Reading 2)

Silence

Short Talk
Less formal exposition. Drama, interviews, testimonies,
discussion, stories, illustrations or audio-visuals could be
used within the talk or in between parts of the talk.

8 *Response and Worship*

Songs I bow my knee before your throne (*The Source*)
Beauty for ashes (*The Source 2*)
Standing in your presence (*The Source 2*)

Stand

We say together in faith
Holy, holy, holy
is the Lord God almighty,
who was, and is, and is to come.

We believe in God the Father,
who created all things:
for by his will they were created
and have their being.

Soft music introduction to the song 'Just let me say' begins at the start of the Absolution.

Music ends.

The reading(s) follow unannounced.

Talk linked to the overall theme if there is one. Challenging and affirming, giving practical help for discipleship. Contemporary and relevant, linking with everyday life.

Worship leader to introduce this time of sung worship and response. Guidance as to how people might respond through the worship could be given. Songs linked using instrumental music.

Music ends.

We believe in God the Son,
who was slain:
for with his blood,
he purchased us for God,
from every tribe and language,
from every people and nation.

We believe in God the Holy Spirit:
the Spirit and the Bride say, 'Come!'
Even so come, Lord Jesus! Amen.

9 *Intercessory Worship*

Sung worship providing the framework for, or leading into open prayer (prayers offered by the congregation either silently or aloud).

After the singing of 'All who are thirsty', space could be left for open prayer along the themes given in the headings – prayer could be directed by headings projected onto a screen. Alternatively, a prayer leader could guide through spoken or written prayers leaving space for open prayer. After the prayers the chorus of 'All who are thirsty' could be repeated. In some churches this form of open prayer may lead to the sharing of prophecies and other spiritual gifts. Some gifted musicians or members of the congregation may be able to sing prayers or prophecies. Projected images, artwork, dance and signing could also be used creatively within this section of the service.

Song All who are thirsty (*The Source 2*)

- Prayer for the church
- Prayer for the world, leaders and our nation
- Prayer for your local community
- Prayer for the suffering and those in need

Song All who are thirsty (chorus)

Sensitive background music could continue.

To conclude the time of intercession a musical introduction leads into the singing of 'All who are thirsty'.

10 *The Peace*

Peace to you from God our heavenly Father.
Peace from his Son Jesus Christ who is our peace.
Peace from the Holy Spirit, the life-giver.
The peace of the triune God be always with you.

The peace of the Lord be always with you.
and also with you.

Song The Lord is present here (*The Source 2*)

After singing the song instrumental music continues softly in the background during the Eucharistic prayer.

11 *Eucharistic Prayer (E)*

The Lord be with you
and also with you.

Lift up your hearts.
We lift them to the Lord.

Let us give thanks to the Lord our God.
It is right to give thanks and praise.

It is indeed right, our duty and our joy,
always and everywhere to give you thanks,
holy Father, almighty and eternal God.
For with your only-begotten Son and the Holy Spirit
you are one God, one Lord.
All that you reveal of your glory,
the same we believe of the Son
and of the Holy Spirit,
without any difference or inequality.
We, your holy Church, acclaim you,
Father of majesty unbounded,
your true and only Son, worthy of all worship,
and the Holy Spirit, advocate and guide.
Three Persons we adore,
one in being and equal in majesty.
And so with angels and archangels,
with cherubim and seraphim,
we sing for ever of your glory:

Song The Lord is present here (chorus)

We praise and bless you, loving Father,
through Jesus Christ, our Lord;
and as we obey his command,
send your Holy Spirit,
that broken bread and wine outpoured
may be for us the body and blood of your dear Son.

On the night before he died
he had supper with his friends
and, taking bread, he praised you.
He broke the bread, gave it to them and said:
Take, eat; this is my body which is given for you;
do this in remembrance of me.

When supper was ended he took the cup of wine.
Again he praised you, gave it to them and said:
Drink this, all of you;
this is my blood of the new covenant,
which is shed for you and for many
for the forgiveness of sins.
Do this, as often as you drink it,
in remembrance of me.

So, Father, we remember all that Jesus did,
in him we plead with confidence his sacrifice
made once for all upon the cross.
Bringing before you the bread of life and cup of salvation,
we proclaim his death and resurrection
until he comes in glory.

Christ has died
Christ is risen
Christ will come again.

Lord of all life,
help us to work together for that day
when your kingdom comes
and justice and mercy will be seen in all the earth.

The background music develops into a
clear introduction for the chorus of the
forthcoming song.

Music ends.

Look with favour on your people,
gather us in your loving arms
and bring us with [N and] all the saints
to feast at your table in heaven.

Through Christ, and with Christ, and in Christ,
in the unity of the Holy Spirit,
all honour and glory are yours, O loving Father,
for ever and ever.
Amen.

12 *Breaking of the Bread*

The president breaks the consecrated bread.

We break this bread
to share in the body of Christ.
**Though we are many, we are one body,
because we all share in one bread.**

13 *Giving of Communion*

The president invites the congregation to receive Communion.

The president and people receive Communion.

Songs Friend of sinners (*The Source 2*)
O sacred King (*The Bridge*)
I thank you for the precious blood (*The Source 2*)
You are the sovereign 'I Am' (*The Source 2*)

Prayer ministry could also be made available during communion.

Songs are linked using instrumental music. As communion progresses the music builds into a time of thanksgiving and proclamation with the final two songs.

Before the Blessing offer the opportunity for prayer ministry following the Dismissal.

14 *The Blessing and Dismissal*

God the Holy Trinity make you strong in faith and love,
defend you on every side,
and guide you in truth and peace;
and the blessing of God almighty,
the Father, the Son, and the Holy Spirit,
be among you and remain with you always.
Amen.

Go in the peace of Christ. Alleluia, Alleluia.
Thanks be to God. Alleluia, Alleluia.

15 *Prayer Ministry Available*

Soft worship music could be played or sung as people leave or as prayer continues.

Third Sunday after Trinity
Service of Holy Communion

Order of Service

Directions

1 The Gathering

Worship songs reflecting a call to worship to be played
as people enter or as refreshments are served before the
service. People should be free to greet each other, sit
quietly or join in with the songs.

Song suggestions for a call to worship
All who are thirsty (*The Source 2*)
Come, now is the time to worship (*The Source 2*)
Praise the Lord (Lomax) (*The Source 2*)

Songs led by worship band or music group.

2 Welcome and Introduction

*Warm and inviting. Visitors and newcomers
should be made particularly welcome. A
clear verbal outline of the service could be
given.*

Stand

Opening song He is the Lord (*The Source*)

SHORT PAUSE

3 Prayer of Preparation

> **Almighty God,**
> **to whom all hearts are open,**
> **all desires known,**
> **and from whom no secrets are hidden:**
> **cleanse the thoughts of our hearts**
> **by the inspiration of your Holy Spirit,**
> **that we may perfectly love you,**
> **and worthily magnify your holy name;**
> **through Christ our Lord. Amen.**

*Extended music introduction to 'There is
freedom at the cross' begins during the
prayer of preparation.*

Song There is freedom at the cross (v 1 and chorus)
    (*The Source 2*)

*After the prayer move directly into the
song.*

Sit if not already doing so.

4 Prayers of Penitence

Sensitive background music continues.

The Summary of the Law

> Our Lord Jesus Christ said:
> The first commandment is this:
> 'Hear, O Israel, the Lord our God is the only Lord.
> You shall love the Lord your God with all your heart,
> with all your soul, with all your mind,
> and with all your strength.'

> The second is this: 'Love your neighbour as yourself.'
> There is no other commandment greater than these.
> On these two commandments hang all the law
> and the prophets.

> **Amen. Lord, have mercy.**

Invitation to confession

> God so loved the world
> that he gave his only Son Jesus Christ
> to save us from our sins,
> to be our advocate in heaven,
> and to bring us to eternal life.
>
> Let us confess our sins in penitence and faith,
> firmly resolved to keep God's commandments
> and to live in love and peace with all.
>
> **My God, for love of you**
> **I desire to hate and forsake all sins**
> **by which I have ever displeased you;**
> **and I resolve by the help of your grace**
> **to commit them no more;**
> **and to avoid all opportunities of sin.**
> **Help me to do this, through Jesus Christ our Lord.**
> **Amen.**

The president says

> May the Father of all mercies
> cleanse *us* from *our* sins,
> and restore *us* in his image
> to the praise and glory of his name,
> through Jesus Christ our Lord.
> **Amen.**

Song There is freedom at the cross (v 2 and chorus)
(*The Source 2*)

During the Absolution the background music develops into an introduction to the approaching song.

After the song the music ends.

5 **The Collect**

> Almighty God,
> you have broken the tyranny of sin
> and have sent the Spirit of your Son into our hearts
> whereby we call you Father:
> give us grace to dedicate our freedom to your service,
> that we and all creation may be brought
> to the glorious liberty of the children of God;
> through Jesus Christ your Son our Lord,
> who is alive and reigns with you,
> in the unity of the Holy Spirit,
> one God, now and for ever.
> **Amen**.

Silence

Stand

6 **Extended Time of Sung Worship**

Songs The Lord is present here (*The Source 2*)
Your eye is on the sparrow (*The Source 2*)
This is the air I breathe (*The Source 2*)

Songs linked with instrumental music.

7 *Open Worship*

(Open to God, open prayer or praise, reflecting, sharing gifts of the Spirit)

Sensitive instrumental music continues in the background. Open to the Holy Spirit. It may be appropriate to encourage the congregation to be free in their expression of worship at this point (e.g. to speak out prayer or to pray silently). It is important for the worship leader to direct worship sensitively at this point.

Music ends.

Silence

8 *The Liturgy of the Word*
First Reading

The reading follows unannounced.

Silence

Gospel Reading
When the Gospel is announced the reader says

Hear the Gospel of our Lord Jesus Christ according to *N.*
Glory to you, O Lord.

Following the reading

This is the Gospel of the Lord.
Praise to you, O Christ.

Silence

Sermon
Less formal exposition. Drama, interviews, testimonies, discussion, stories, illustrations or audio-visuals could be used within the sermon or in between parts of the sermon.

Sermon linked to the overall theme if there is one. Challenging and affirming, giving practical help for discipleship. Contemporary and relevant, linking with everyday life.

Silence

Silence used to reflect on the Sermon.

Ministry song played live or from a CD to the congregation. (Images to accompany the song could be projected onto the screen. Mime or dance could be performed.)

Stand

9 *The Nicene Creed*

We believe in one God,
the Father, the Almighty,
maker of heaven and earth,
of all that is, seen and unseen.

We believe in one Lord, Jesus Christ,
the only Son of God,
eternally begotten of the Father,
God from God, Light from Light,
true God from true God,
begotten, not made,
of one Being with the Father;
through him all things were made.
For us and for our salvation
he came down from heaven,
was incarnate from the Holy Spirit

and the Virgin Mary
and was made man.
**For our sake he was crucified under Pontius Pilate;
he suffered death and was buried.
On the third day he rose again
in accordance with the Scriptures;
he ascended into heaven
and is seated at the right hand of the Father.
He will come again in glory
to judge the living and the dead,
and his kingdom will have no end.**

**We believe in the Holy Spirit,
the Lord, the giver of life,
who proceeds from the Father and the Son,
who with the Father and the Son
is worshipped and glorified,
who has spoken through the prophets.
We believe in one holy catholic and apostolic Church.
We acknowledge one baptism
for the forgiveness of sins.
We look for the resurrection of the dead,
and the life of the world to come.
Amen.**

10 *Prayers of Intercession*

One person may lead the prayers verbally but other more creative forms of prayer could be used, e.g. visual prayer using projected images as prayer guides, group prayer or open prayer in which people are free to pray their own prayers either silently or aloud. Alternatively, intercessory worship could be used, in which songs provide the framework for open prayer, guided by the worship or service leader. Prophecies and other spiritual gifts could be expressed. Artwork, dance and signing could also be used creatively within this section of the service.

The prayers may follow this sequence:

- The Church of Christ
- Creation, human society, the Sovereign and those in authority
- The local community
- Those who suffer
- The communion of saints

The following response may be used to conclude sections of prayer:

Lord, in your mercy
hear our prayer.

And at the end of the prayers:

Merciful Father,
**accept these prayers
for the sake of your Son,
our Saviour Jesus Christ.
Amen.**

11 *The Liturgy of the Sacrament*

The Peace

Invite the congregation to stand.

> We are all one in Christ Jesus.
> We belong to him through faith,
> heirs of the promise of the Spirit of peace.

> The peace of the Lord be always with you
> **and also with you.**

Let us offer one another a sign of peace.

All may exchange a sign of peace.

Hymn Father, to you (vv 1 and 2) (*The Source 2*)

12 *Eucharistic Prayer (D)*

> The Lord be with you
> **and also with you.**

> Lift up your hearts.
> **We lift them to the Lord.**

> Let us give thanks to the Lord our God.
> **It is right to give thanks and praise.**

> Almighty God, good Father to us all,
> your face is turned towards your world.
> In love you gave us Jesus your Son
> to rescue us from sin and death.
> Your Word goes out to call us home
> to the city where angels sing your praise.
> We join with them in heaven's song:

> **Holy, holy, holy Lord,**
> **God of power and might,**
> **heaven and earth are full of your glory.**
> **Hosanna in the highest.**
> **[Blessed is he who comes in the name of the Lord.**
> **Hosanna in the highest.]**

> Father of all, we give you thanks
> for every gift that comes from heaven.

> To the darkness Jesus came as your light.
> With signs of faith and words of hope
> he touched untouchables with love
> and washed the guilty clean.

> This is his story.
> **This is our song:**
> **Hosanna in the highest.**

> The crowds came out to see your Son,
> yet at the end they turned on him.
> On the night he was betrayed
> he came to table with his friends
> to celebrate the freedom of your people.

> This is his story.
> **This is our song:**
> **Hosanna in the highest.**

Soft music continues in the background to the Eucharistic Prayer.

Jesus blessed you, Father, for the food;
he took bread, gave thanks, broke it and said:
This is my body, given for you all.
Jesus then gave thanks for the wine;
he took the cup, gave it and said:
This is my blood, shed for you all
for the forgiveness of sins.
Do this in remembrance of me.

This is our story.
This is our song:
Hosanna in the highest.

Therefore, Father, with this bread and this cup
we celebrate the cross
on which he died to set us free.
Defying death he rose again
and is alive with you to plead for us and all the world.

This is our story.
This is our song:
Hosanna in the highest.

Send your Spirit on us now
that by these gifts we may feed on Christ
with opened eyes and hearts on fire.

May we and all who share this food
offer ourselves to live for you
and be welcomed at your feast in heaven
where all creation worships you,
Father, Son and Holy Spirit:

Blessing and honour and glory and power
be yours for ever and ever.
Amen.

Song Father, to you (v 3 and chorus)

13 *The Lord's Prayer*

As our Saviour taught us, so we pray

Our Father in heaven,
hallowed be your name,
your kingdom come,
your will be done,
on earth as in heaven.
Give us today our daily bread.
Forgive us our sins
as we forgive those who sin against us.
Lead us not into temptation
but deliver us from evil.
For the kingdom, the power, and the glory are yours
now and for ever.
Amen.

14 *Breaking of the Bread*

The president breaks the consecrated bread.

Towards the end of the Eucharistic Prayer the background music leads into a clear and bold introduction to the final verse of 'Father to you'.

Music ends.

Every time we eat this bread
and drink this cup,
**we proclaim the Lord's death
until he comes.**

15 *Giving of Communion*

The president says the invitation to Communion

God's holy gifts
for God's holy people.
**Jesus Christ is holy, Jesus Christ is Lord,
to the glory of God the Father.**

**We do not presume
to come to this your table, merciful Lord,
trusting in our own righteousness,
but in your manifold and great mercies.
We are not worthy
so much as to gather up the crumbs
under your table.
But you are the same Lord
whose nature is always to have mercy.
Grant us therefore, gracious Lord,
so to eat the flesh of your dear Son Jesus Christ
and to drink his blood,
that our sinful bodies may be made clean
by his body
and our souls washed
through his most precious blood,
and that we may evermore dwell in him
and he in us.
Amen.**

The president and people receive Communion.

During Communion the worship band or music group play
instrumental versions of a few songs.

Silence

Music ends.

16 *Prayer after Communion*

O God, whose beauty is beyond our imagining
and whose power we cannot comprehend:
show us your glory as far as we can grasp it,
and shield us from knowing more than we can bear
until we may look upon you without fear;
through Jesus Christ our Saviour.

**You have opened to us the Scriptures, O Christ,
and you have made yourself known
in the breaking of the bread.
Abide with us, we pray,
that, blessed by your royal presence,
we may walk with you
all the days of our life,
and at its end behold you
in the glory of the eternal Trinity,
one God for ever and ever.
Amen.**

Song There is a louder shout to come (*The Source*)

17 *Blessing*

The peace of God,
which passes all understanding,
keep your hearts and minds
in the knowledge and love of God,
and of his Son Jesus Christ our Lord;
and the blessing of God almighty,
the Father, the Son, and the Holy Spirit,
be among you and remain with you always.
Amen.

Go in peace to love and serve the Lord.
In the name of Christ. Amen.

18 *Prayer Ministry Available*

Following the prayer the song 'There is a louder shout to come' is announced.

Before the Blessing and Dismissal offer the opportunity for prayer ministry.

Soft worship music could be played or sung as people leave or as prayer continues.

Sixth Sunday after Trinity
Service of Holy Communion

Order of Service

1 The Gathering

Worship songs reflecting a call to worship/desire for God to be played as people enter or as refreshments are served before the service. People should be free to greet each other, sit quietly or join in with the songs.

Song suggestions for a call to worship
Lord, we've come to worship (*The Source 2*)
We have come to worship the Lord (*The Source 2*)
This is your house (*The Source 2*)

2 Welcome and Introduction

Stand

3 Prayer of Preparation

Almighty God,
to whom all hearts are open,
all desires known,
and from whom no secrets are hidden:
cleanse the thoughts of our hearts
by the inspiration of your Holy Spirit,
that we may perfectly love you,
and worthily magnify your holy name;
through Christ our Lord.
Amen.

4 Extended Time of Sung Worship

Songs Here is the risen Son (*The Source 2*)
Saviour I will sing to you (*Release*)

5 Open Worship

(Open to God, open prayer or praise, reflecting, sharing gifts of the Spirit)

6 Prayers of Penitence

The Summary of the Law

Our Lord Jesus Christ said:
The first commandment is this:
'Hear, O Israel, the Lord our God is the only Lord.
You shall love the Lord your God with all your heart,

Directions

Songs led by worship band or music group.

Warm and inviting. Visitors and newcomers should be made particularly welcome. A clear verbal outline of the service could be given.

SHORT PAUSE

An introduction to the first song begins immediately after the prayer of preparation.

Sensitive instrumental music continues in the background. Open to the Holy Spirit. It may be appropriate to encourage the congregation to be free in their expression of worship at this point (e.g. to speak out prayer or to pray silently). It is important for the worship leader to direct worship sensitively at this point.

Sensitive background music continues.

with all your soul, with all your mind,
and with all your strength.'

The second is this: 'Love your neighbour as yourself.'
There is no other commandment greater than these.
On these two commandments hang all the law
and the prophets.

Amen. Lord, have mercy.

Invitation to confession

God so loved the world
that he gave his only Son Jesus Christ
to save us from our sins,
to be our advocate in heaven,
and to bring us to eternal life.

Let us confess our sins in penitence and faith,
firmly resolved to keep God's commandments
and to live in love and peace with all.

Almighty God, our heavenly Father,
we have sinned against you
and against our neighbour
in thought and word and deed,
through negligence, through weakness,
through our own deliberate fault.
We are truly sorry and repent of all our sins.
For the sake of your Son Jesus Christ,
who died for us, forgive us all that is past
and grant that we may serve you
in newness of life
to the glory of your name. Amen.

The president says

Almighty God,
who forgives all who truly repent,
have mercy upon *you*,
pardon and deliver *you* from all *your* sins,
confirm and strengthen *you* in all goodness,
and keep *you* in life eternal;
through Jesus Christ our Lord.
Amen.

Songs Jesus, what a beautiful name (*The Source*)
The Lord's my shepherd (Townend) (*The Source 2*)

7 *The Collect*

Merciful God,
you have prepared for those who love you
such good things as pass our understanding:
pour into our hearts such love toward you
that we, loving you in all things and above all things,
may obtain your promises,
which exceed all that we can desire;
through Jesus Christ your Son our Lord,
who is alive and reigns with you,
in the unity of the Holy Spirit,
one God, now and for ever.
Amen.

During the Absolution the background music develops into an introduction to the approaching song.

Sensitive background music continues during the Collect.

Silence

8 ***The Liturgy of the Word***
First Reading

Silence

Gospel Reading
When the Gospel is announced the reader says

> Hear the Gospel of our Lord Jesus Christ according to *N.*
> **Glory to you, O Lord.**

Following the gospel reading

> This is the Gospel of the Lord.
> **Praise to you, O Christ.**

Silence

Sermon
Less formal exposition. Drama, interviews, testimonies, discussion, stories, illustrations or audio-visuals could be used within the sermon or in between parts of the sermon.

Silence

Ministry song played live or from a CD to the congregation. (Images to accompany the song could be projected onto the screen. Mime or dance could be performed.)

Stand

9 ***The Nicene Creed***

> **We believe in one God,**
> **the Father, the Almighty,**
> **maker of heaven and earth,**
> **of all that is,**
> **seen and unseen.**
>
> **We believe in one Lord, Jesus Christ,**
> **the only Son of God,**
> **eternally begotten of the Father,**
> **God from God, Light from Light,**
> **true God from true God,**
> **begotten, not made,**
> **of one Being with the Father;**
> **through him all things were made.**
> **For us and for our salvation**
> **he came down from heaven,**
> **was incarnate from the Holy Spirit**
> **and the Virgin Mary**
> **and was made man.**
> **For our sake he was crucified under Pontius Pilate;**
> **he suffered death and was buried.**
> **On the third day he rose again**
> **in accordance with the Scriptures;**
> **he ascended into heaven**
> **and is seated at the right hand of the Father.**
> **He will come again in glory**

Music ends.

The readings follow unannounced.

Sermon linked to the overall theme if there is one. Challenging and affirming, giving practical help for discipleship. Contemporary and relevant, linking with everyday life.

Silence used to reflect on the sermon.

to judge the living and the dead,
and his kingdom will have no end.

We believe in the Holy Spirit,
the Lord, the giver of life,
who proceeds from the Father and the Son,
who with the Father and the Son
is worshipped and glorified,
who has spoken through the prophets.
We believe in one holy catholic and apostolic Church.
We acknowledge one baptism
for the forgiveness of sins.
We look for the resurrection of the dead,
and the life of the world to come.
Amen.

10 *Prayers of Intercession*

One person may lead the prayers verbally but other more creative forms of prayer could be used, e.g. visual prayer using projected images as prayer guides, group prayer or open prayer in which people are free to pray their own prayers either silently or aloud. Alternatively, intercessory worship could be used, in which songs provide the framework for open prayer, guided by the worship or service leader. Prophecies and other spiritual gifts could be expressed. Artwork, dance and signing could also be used creatively within this section of the service.

The prayers may follow this sequence:

- The Church of Christ
- Creation, human society, the Sovereign and those in authority
- The local community
- Those who suffer
- The communion of saints

The following response may be used to conclude sections of prayer:

Lord, in your mercy
hear our prayer.

And at the end of the prayers:

Merciful Father,
**accept these prayers
for the sake of your Son,
our Saviour Jesus Christ.
Amen.**

11 *The Liturgy of the Sacrament*

The Peace

Invite the congregation to stand.

The peace of the Lord be always with you
and also with you.

Let us offer one another a sign of peace.

All may exchange a sign of peace.

Song Should he who made the stars (*The Bridge*)

During the Peace an extended musical introduction to the song is played. The song starts as people have returned to their places.

12 *Eucharistic Prayer (G)*

The Lord be with you
and also with you.

Lift up your hearts.
We lift them to the Lord.

Let us give thanks to the Lord our God.
It is right to give thanks and praise.

Blessed are you, Lord God,
our light and our salvation;
to you be glory and praise for ever.

From the beginning you have created all things
and all your works echo the silent music of your praise.
In the fullness of time you made us in your image,
the crown of all creation.

You give us breath and speech,
that with angels and archangels
and all the powers of heaven
we may find a voice to sing your praise:

Soft music continues in the background to the Eucharistic Prayer.

Background music develops into clear introduction to the chorus of the song.

Song Should he who made the stars (chorus) (*The Source 2*)

Background music continues.

How wonderful the work of your hands, O Lord.
As a mother tenderly gathers her children,
you embraced a people as your own.
When they turned away and rebelled
your love remained steadfast.

From them you raised up Jesus our Saviour,
born of Mary,
to be the living bread,
in whom all our hungers are satisfied.

He offered his life for sinners,
and with a love stronger than death
he opened wide his arms on the cross.

On the night before he died,
he came to supper with his friends
and, taking bread, he gave you thanks.
He broke it and gave it to them, saying:
Take, eat; this is my body which is given for you;
do this in remembrance of me.

At the end of supper, taking the cup of wine,
he gave you thanks, and said:
Drink this, all of you;
this is my blood of the new covenant,
which is shed for you and for many
for the forgiveness of sins.
Do this, as often as you drink it,
in remembrance of me.

Background music develops into clear introduction to the chorus of the song.

Song Should he who made the stars (chorus) (*The Source 2*)

Father, we plead with confidence
his sacrifice made once for all upon the cross;
we remember his dying and rising in glory,
and we rejoice that he intercedes for us
at your right hand.

Pour out your Holy Spirit as we bring before you
these gifts of your creation;
may they be for us the body and blood
of your dear Son.

As we eat and drink these holy things in your presence,
form us in the likeness of Christ,
and build us into a living temple to your glory.

Bring us at the last with [*N and*] all the saints
to the vision of that eternal splendour
for which you have created us;
through Jesus Christ, our Lord,
by whom, with whom, and in whom,
with all who stand before you in earth and heaven,
we worship you, Father almighty,
in songs of everlasting praise:

**Blessing and honour and glory and power
be yours for ever and ever.
Amen.**

Song Should he who made the stars (chorus) (*The Source 2*)

13 *Breaking of the Bread*

The president breaks the consecrated bread.

Every time we eat this bread
and drink this cup,
**we proclaim the Lord's death
until he comes.**

14 *Giving of Communion*

The president says the invitation to Communion

God's holy gifts
for God's holy people.
**Jesus Christ is holy,
Jesus Christ is Lord,
to the glory of God the Father.**

**We do not presume
to come to this your table, merciful Lord,
trusting in our own righteousness,
but in your manifold and great mercies.
We are not worthy
so much as to gather up the crumbs
under your table.
But you are the same Lord
whose nature is always to have mercy.
Grant us therefore, gracious Lord,**

Background music continues.

Background music develops into clear introduction to the chorus of the song.

Music ends.

**so to eat the flesh of your dear Son Jesus Christ
and to drink his blood,
that our sinful bodies may be made clean
by his body
and our souls washed
through his most precious blood,
and that we may evermore dwell in him
and he in us.
Amen.**

The president and people receive Communion.

Songs/Hymns during Communion
When I survey (*The Source*)
Thank you for saving me (*The Source*)
This is the air I breathe (*The Source 2*)

Silence

15 *Prayer after Communion*

God of our pilgrimage,
you have led us to the living water:
refresh and sustain us
as we go forward on our journey,
in the name of Jesus Christ our Lord.

**Almighty God,
we thank you for feeding us
with the body and blood of your Son Jesus Christ.
Through him we offer you our souls and bodies
to be a living sacrifice.
Send us out in the power of your Spirit
to live and work to your praise and glory.
Amen.**

Hymn All for Jesus! (*The Bridge*)

16 *Blessing*

May God, who in Christ
gives us a spring of water welling up to eternal life,
perfect in you the image of his glory;
and the blessing of God almighty,
the Father, the Son, and the Holy Spirit,
be among you and remain with you always.
Amen.

Go in the peace of Christ.
Thanks be to God.

Song The Grace (*The Source 2*)

17 *Prayer Ministry Available*

Songs and hymns linked with instrumental music.

Music ends.

After the prayer the hymn is announced.

Before the Blessing and Dismissal offer the opportunity for prayer ministry.

The singing of the Grace is announced.

Soft worship music could be played or sung as people leave or as prayer continues.

Ninth Sunday after Trinity
Service of Holy Communion

Order of Service

1 Welcome and Introduction

Warm and inviting. Visitors and newcomers should be made particularly welcome. A clear verbal outline of the service could be given.

SHORT PAUSE

Stand

2 Prayer of Preparation

**Almighty God,
to whom all hearts are open,
all desires known,
and from whom no secrets are hidden:
cleanse the thoughts of our hearts
by the inspiration of your Holy Spirit,
that we may perfectly love you,
and worthily magnify your holy name;
through Christ our Lord.
Amen.**

3 Extended Time of Sung Worship

Songs Great is the Lord (*The Source*)
To the King eternal (*The Source 2*)
O, the love of God is boundless (vv 1-3)
(*The Source 2*)

An introduction to the first song begins immediately after the prayer of preparation.

Songs linked with instrumental music.

Sit if not already doing so.

4 Prayers of Penitence

Invitation to confession

God so loved the world
that he gave his only Son Jesus Christ
to save us from our sins,
to be our advocate in heaven,
and to bring us to eternal life.

Let us confess our sins in penitence and faith,
firmly resolved to keep God's commandments
and to live in love and peace with all.

Sensitive background music continues during the Prayers of Penitence.

**Almighty God,
long-suffering and of great goodness:
I confess to you,
I confess with my whole heart
my neglect and forgetfulness
of your commandments,
my wrong doing, thinking, and speaking;
the hurts I have done to others,
and the good I have left undone.
O God, forgive me, for I have sinned against you;
and raise me to newness of life;
through Jesus Christ our Lord.
Amen.**

The president says
> May almighty God,
> who sent his Son into the world to save sinners,
> bring *you* his pardon and peace,
> now and for ever.
> **Amen**.

Song O, the love of God is boundless (v 4) (*The Source 2*)

5 *Open Worship*
(Open to God, open prayer or praise, reflecting, sharing gifts of the Spirit)

Silence

6 *The Collect*
> Almighty God,
> who sent your Holy Spirit
> to be the life and light of your Church:
> open our hearts to the riches of your grace,
> that we may bring forth the fruit of the Spirit
> in love and joy and peace;
> through Jesus Christ your Son our Lord.
>
> **Amen.**

7 *The Liturgy of the Word*
First Reading

Silence

Gospel Reading
> Alleluia, alleluia.
> Speak, Lord, for your servant is listening.
> You have the words of eternal life.
> **Alleluia.**

When the Gospel is announced the reader says
> Hear the Gospel of our Lord Jesus Christ according to *N*.
> **Glory to you, O Lord.**

Following the gospel reading
> This is the Gospel of the Lord.
> **Praise to you, O Christ.**

Silence

Sermon
Less formal exposition. Drama, interviews, testimonies, discussion, stories, illustrations or audio-visuals could be used within the Sermon or in between parts of the Sermon.

Silence

During the Absolution the background instrumental music develops into a bold introduction for the approaching song.

Sensitive instrumental music continues in the background. Open to the Holy Spirit. It may be appropriate to encourage the congregation to be free in their expression of worship at this point (e.g. to speak out prayer or to pray silently). It is important for the worship leader to direct worship sensitively at this point.

The music ends after the time of open worship.

The reading follows unannounced.

Sermon linked to the overall theme if there is one. Challenging and affirming, giving practical help for discipleship. Contemporary and relevant, linking with everyday life.

Silence used to reflect on the Sermon.

8 *Response*

Prior to the service resources needed for the response should be prepared and set up. In one area of the church an ironing board is needed and hanging over it a washing line, on which a large number of pegs are placed. In another area of church a rope hanging loosely from a beam (or ceiling) and under it a large number of small rocks or stones. In the third area a table on which an empty champagne bottle is placed. A large number of corks are placed around the bottle.

The congregation is invited to respond to God's call in one of the following ways.

1. To accept the call to love and serve God in the ordinary things and in everyday life by taking a peg from the washing line.

2. To accept the call to be a pioneer and to rise to the challenge of living an adventure for God by taking a rock from under the rope.

3. To celebrate the fact that you are called, chosen and loved by God by taking one of the corks around the champagne bottle.

The peg, rock or cork are to act as a reminder of the response each person makes. People are free to keep them and take them home.

Before the time of response ends you may wish to pray for everyone as they hold the response object of their choice.

Suggested songs during the response:
How lovely is your dwelling place (*The Source 2*)
O that you would bless me (*The Bridge*)
Hungry I come to you (*The Source 2*)

Stand

9 **The Nicene Creed**

> **We believe in one God,**
> **the Father, the Almighty,**
> **maker of heaven and earth,**
> **of all that is, seen and unseen.**
>
> **We believe in one Lord, Jesus Christ,**
> **the only Son of God,**
> **eternally begotten of the Father,**
> **God from God, Light from Light,**
> **true God from true God,**
> **begotten, not made,**
> **of one Being with the Father;**
> **through him all things were made.**
> **For us and for our salvation**
> **he came down from heaven,**
> **was incarnate from the Holy Spirit**
> **and the Virgin Mary**
> **and was made man.**
> **For our sake he was crucified under Pontius Pilate;**

Sung worship continues during the response.

Songs linked with extended times of instrumental music.

After the response the music ends.

he suffered death and was buried.
On the third day he rose again
in accordance with the Scriptures;
he ascended into heaven
and is seated at the right hand of the Father.
He will come again in glory
to judge the living and the dead,
and his kingdom will have no end.

We believe in the Holy Spirit,
the Lord, the giver of life,
who proceeds from the Father and the Son,
who with the Father and the Son
is worshipped and glorified,
who has spoken through the prophets.
We believe in one holy catholic and apostolic Church.
We acknowledge one baptism
for the forgiveness of sins.
We look for the resurrection of the dead,
and the life of the world to come.
Amen.

10 *Prayers of Intercession*

One person may lead the prayers verbally but other more creative forms of prayer could be used, e.g. visual prayer using projected images as prayer guides, group prayer or open prayer in which people are free to pray their own prayers either silently or aloud. Alternatively, intercessory worship could be used, in which songs provide the framework for open prayer, guided by the worship or service leader. Prophecies and other spiritual gifts could be expressed. Artwork, dance and signing could also be used creatively within this section of the service.

The prayers may follow this sequence:
- The Church of Christ
- Creation, human society, the Sovereign and those in authority
- The local community
- Those who suffer
- The communion of saints

The following response may be used to conclude sections of prayer:

Lord, in your mercy
hear our prayer.

And at the end of the prayers:

Merciful Father,
**accept these prayers
for the sake of your Son,
our Saviour Jesus Christ.
Amen.**

11 *The Liturgy of the Sacrament*

The Peace

Invite the congregation to stand.

'Where two or three are gathered together in my name,'
says the Lord, 'there am I in the midst of them.'

The peace of the Lord be always with you
and also with you.

Let us offer one another a sign of peace.

All may exchange a sign of peace.

Hymn Thine be the glory (*The Source*)

12 *Eucharistic Prayer (H)*

The Lord be with you
and also with you.

Lift up your hearts.
We lift them to the Lord.

Let us give thanks to the Lord our God.
It is right to give thanks and praise.

It is right to praise you, Father, Lord of all creation;
in your love you made us for yourself.

When we turned away
you did not reject us,
but came to meet us in your Son.
**You embraced us as your children
and welcomed us to sit and eat with you.**

In Christ you shared our life
that we might live in him and he in us.
**He opened his arms of love upon the cross
and made for all the perfect sacrifice for sin.**

On the night he was betrayed,
at supper with his friends
he took bread, and gave you thanks;
he broke it and gave it to them, saying:
Take, eat; this is my body which is given for you;
do this in remembrance of me.
**Father, we do this in remembrance of him:
his body is the bread of life.**

At the end of supper, taking the cup of wine,
he gave you thanks, and said:
Drink this, all of you;
this is my blood of the new covenant,
which is shed for you for the forgiveness of sins;
do this in remembrance of me.
**Father, we do this in remembrance of him:
his blood is shed for all.**

As we proclaim his death
and celebrate his rising in glory,
send your Holy Spirit that this bread and this wine
may be to us the body and blood of your dear Son.

After the Peace the hymn is announced.

Music from the hymn continues softly in
the background to the Eucharistic Prayer.

**As we eat and drink these holy gifts
make us one in Christ, our risen Lord.**

With your whole Church throughout the world
we offer you this sacrifice of praise
and lift our voice to join the eternal song of heaven:

**Holy, holy, holy Lord,
God of power and might,
Heaven and earth are full of your glory.
Hosanna in the highest.**

Hymn Thine be the glory

13 *Breaking of the Bread*

The president breaks the consecrated bread.

**Lamb of God,
you take away the sin of the world,
have mercy on us.**

**Lamb of God,
you take away the sin of the world,
have mercy on us.**

**Lamb of God,
you take away the sin of the world,
grant us peace.**

14 *Giving of Communion*

The president says the invitation to Communion

Jesus is the Lamb of God
who takes away the sin of the world.
Blessed are those who are called to his supper.
**Lord, I am not worthy to receive you,
but only say the word, and I shall be healed.**

**Most merciful Lord,
your love compels us to come in.
Our hands were unclean,
our hearts were unprepared;
we were not fit even to eat the crumbs
from under your table.
But you, Lord, are the God of our salvation,
and share your bread with sinners.
So cleanse and feed us
with the precious body and blood of your Son,
that he may live in us and we in him;
and that we, with the whole company of Christ,
may sit and eat in your kingdom.
Amen.**

The president and people receive Communion.

Songs/Hymns during Communion:
Beauty for ashes (*The Source 2*)
Breathe on me Breath of God (*The Source*)
I thank you for the precious blood of Jesus (*The Source 2*)

During 'holy, holy, holy . . .' the background music develops into a clear and bold introduction to the chorus of the hymn.

Music ends.

Towards the end of the giving of Communion the music and sung worship grows in strength and develops into joyful songs of thanksgiving.

Stand

15 Sung Time of Thanksgiving

Songs/Hymns

Your love is amazing (*The Source 2*)
Thank you for saving me (*The Source*)
To God be the glory (*The Source*)

16 Prayer after Communion

Holy Father,
who gathered us here around the table of your Son
to share this meal with the whole household of God:
in that new world
where you reveal the fullness of your peace,
gather people of every race and language
to share in the eternal banquet of Jesus Christ our Lord.

**Faithful God,
in baptism you have adopted us as your children,
made us members of the body of Christ
and chosen us as inheritors of your kingdom:
we thank you that in this Eucharist
you renew your promises within us,
empower us by your Spirit to witness and to serve,
and send us out as disciples of your Son,
Jesus Christ our Lord.
Amen.**

17 Blessing

God the Father,
by whose glory Christ was raised from the dead,
strengthen you to walk with him in his risen life;
and the blessing of God almighty,
the Father, the Son, and the Holy Spirit,
be among you and remain with you always.
Amen.

Go in the peace of Christ.
Thanks be to God.

Song The Grace (*The Source 2*)

18 Prayer Ministry Available

Before the Blessing and Dismissal offer the opportunity for prayer ministry.

The singing of the Grace is announced.

Soft worship music could be played or sung as people leave or as prayer continues.

Twelfth Sunday after Trinity
Service of Holy Communion

Order of Service

1 The Gathering

Worship songs reflecting a call to worship to be played as people enter or as refreshments are served before the service. People should be free to greet each other, sit quietly or join in with the songs.

Song suggestions for a call to worship
Lord, we've come to worship (*The Source 2*)
Lord, we come to seek your face (*The Source 2*)
We've come to praise your name (*Release*)

2 Welcome and Introduction

Stand

3 Prayer of Preparation

Almighty God,
to whom all hearts are open,
all desires known,
and from whom no secrets are hidden:
cleanse the thoughts of our hearts
by the inspiration of your Holy Spirit,
that we may perfectly love you,
and worthily magnify your holy name;
through Christ our Lord.
Amen.

4 Extended Time of Sung Worship Including Confession

Songs I will give thanks to thee (*The Source 2*)
Praise the Lord (Lomax) (*The Source 2*)

5 Open Worship

(Open to God, open prayer or praise, reflecting, sharing gifts of the Spirit)

Song I lift my eyes up to the mountains (*The Source*)

Directions

Songs led by worship band or music group.

Warm and inviting. Visitors and newcomers should be made particularly welcome. A clear verbal outline of the service could be given.

After the Prayer of Preparation, move directly into the first song.

The song 'Praise the Lord' should be sung boldly but could be sung more gently to finish. The final phrase of the song, 'praise the Lord', could be sung several times.

Sensitive instrumental music continues in the background. Open to the Holy Spirit. It may be appropriate to encourage the congregation to be free in their expression of worship at this point (e.g. to speak out prayer or to pray silently). It is important for the worship leader to direct worship sensitively at this point.

At an appropriate point after the Open Worship, the music develops into a clear introduction to the next song.

Sit if not already doing so.

6 Confession

Invitation to confession
Let us then approach the throne of grace with confidence, so that we may receive mercy and find grace to help us in our time of need. (Hebrews 4:16)

Song Before the throne of God above (vv 1 and 2) (*The Source 2*)

Silence

> We say together:
>
> Lord our God,
> in our sin we have avoided your call.
> Our love for you is like a morning cloud,
> like the dew that goes away early.
> Have mercy on us;
> deliver us from judgement;
> bind up our wounds
> and revive us;
> in Jesus Christ our Lord. Amen.

The minister says

> The Lord forgive *you your* sin,
> unite *you* in the love which took Christ to the cross,
> and bring *you* in the Spirit to his wedding feast in heaven.
> **Amen.**

Invite the congregation to stand.

Song Before the throne of God above (v 3) (*The Source 2*)

Sit

Silence

7 The Collect

> Almighty and everlasting God,
> you are always more ready to hear than we to pray
> and to give more than either we desire or deserve:
> pour down upon us the abundance of your mercy,
> forgiving us those things
> of which our conscience is afraid
> and giving us those good things
> which we are not worthy to ask
> but through the merits and mediation
> of Jesus Christ your Son our Lord.
> **Amen.**

8 The Liturgy of the Word
First Reading

Silence

The music ends for the Invitation to Confession.

The song begins unannounced.

Music ends.

A clear and bold introduction to the final verse of 'Before the throne of God above' starts.

Music ends.

The reading follows unannounced.

Gospel Reading

When the Gospel is announced the reader says

> Hear the Gospel of our Lord Jesus Christ according to *N*.
> **Glory to you, O Lord.**

Following the Gospel

> This is the Gospel of the Lord
> **Praise to you, O Christ.**

Silence

Sermon

Less formal exposition. Drama, interviews, testimonies, discussion, stories, illustrations or audio-visuals could be used within the sermon or in between parts of the sermon.

Silence

Ministry song played live or from a CD to the congregation. (Images to accompany the song could be projected onto the screen. Mime or dance could be performed.)

Stand

9   *The Nicene Creed*

> **We believe in one God,**
> **the Father, the Almighty,**
> **maker of heaven and earth,**
> **of all that is,**
> **seen and unseen.**
>
> **We believe in one Lord, Jesus Christ,**
> **the only Son of God,**
> **eternally begotten of the Father,**
> **God from God, Light from Light,**
> **true God from true God,**
> **begotten, not made,**
> **of one Being with the Father;**
> **through him all things were made.**
> **For us and for our salvation**
> **he came down from heaven,**
> **was incarnate from the Holy Spirit**
> **and the Virgin Mary**
> **and was made man.**
> **For our sake he was crucified under Pontius Pilate;**
> **he suffered death and was buried.**
> **On the third day he rose again**
> **in accordance with the Scriptures;**
> **he ascended into heaven**
> **and is seated at the right hand of the Father.**
> **He will come again in glory**
> **to judge the living and the dead,**
> **and his kingdom will have no end.**
>
> **We believe in the Holy Spirit,**
> **the Lord, the giver of life,**
> **who proceeds from the Father and the Son,**
> **who with the Father and the Son**

Sermon linked to the overall theme if there is one. Challenging and affirming, giving practical help for discipleship. Contemporary and relevant, linking with everyday life.

Silence used to reflect on the Sermon.

**is worshipped and glorified,
who has spoken through the prophets.
We believe in one holy catholic and apostolic Church.
We acknowledge one baptism
for the forgiveness of sins.
We look for the resurrection of the dead,
and the life of the world to come.
Amen.**

10 *Prayers of Intercession*

One person may lead the prayers verbally but other more creative forms of prayer could be used, e.g. visual prayer using projected images as prayer guides, group prayer or open prayer in which people are free to pray their own prayers either silently or aloud. Alternatively, intercessory worship could be used, in which songs provide the framework for open prayer, guided by the worship or service leader. Prophecies and other spiritual gifts could be expressed. Artwork, dance and signing could also be used creatively within this section of the service.

The prayers may follow this sequence:

- The Church of Christ
- Creation, human society, the Sovereign and those in authority
- The local community
- Those who suffer
- The communion of saints

The following response may be used to conclude sections of prayer:

Lord, in your mercy
hear our prayer.

And at the end of the prayers:

Merciful Father,
**accept these prayers
for the sake of your Son,
our Saviour Jesus Christ.
Amen.**

11 *The Liturgy of the Sacrament*

The Peace

Invite the congregation to stand.

We are all one in Christ Jesus.
We belong to him through faith,
heirs of the promise of the Spirit of peace.

The peace of the Lord be always with you
and also with you.

Let us offer one another a sign of peace.

All may exchange a sign of peace.

Hymn Christ is made the sure foundation (vv 1, 2 and 3)
(*The Source 2*)

The hymn is announced.

12 *Eucharistic Prayer (B)*

The Lord be with you
and also with you.

Lift up your hearts.
We lift them to the Lord.

Let us give thanks to the Lord our God.
It is right to give thanks and praise.

It is truly right and just, our duty and our salvation,
always and everywhere to give you thanks,
holy Father, almighty and eternal God.
From sunrise to sunset this day is holy,
for Christ has risen from the tomb
and scattered the darkness of death
with light that will not fade.
This day the risen Lord walks with your gathered people,
unfolds for us your word,
and makes himself known in the breaking of the bread.
And though the night will overtake this day
you summon us to live in endless light,
the never-ceasing sabbath of the Lord.
And so, with choirs of angels
and with all the heavenly host,
we proclaim your glory
and join their unending song of praise:

Holy, holy, holy Lord,
God of power and might,
heaven and earth are full of your glory.
Hosanna in the highest.

Lord, you are holy indeed, the source of all holiness;
grant that by the power of your Holy Spirit,
and according to your holy will,
these gifts of bread and wine
may be to us the body and blood of our Lord Jesus Christ;

who, in the same night that he was betrayed,
took bread and gave you thanks;
he broke it and gave it to his disciples, saying:
Take, eat; this is my body which is given for you;
do this in remembrance of me.

In the same way, after supper
he took the cup and gave you thanks;
he gave it to them, saying:
Drink this, all of you;
this is my blood of the new covenant,
which is shed for you and for many
for the forgiveness of sins.
Do this, as often as you drink it,
in remembrance of me.

Jesus Christ is Lord:
Lord, by your cross and resurrection
you have set us free.
You are the Saviour of the world.

And so, Father, calling to mind his death on the cross,
his perfect sacrifice made once

Soft music continues in the background to
the Eucharistic Prayer.

for the sins of the whole world;
rejoicing in his mighty resurrection and glorious ascension,
and looking for his coming in glory,
we celebrate this memorial of our redemption.
As we offer you this our sacrifice
of praise and thanksgiving,
we bring before you this bread and this cup
and we thank you for counting us worthy
to stand in your presence and serve you.

Send the Holy Spirit on your people
and gather into one in your kingdom
all who share this one bread and one cup,
so that we, in the company of [N and] all the saints,
may praise and glorify you for ever,
through Jesus Christ our Lord;

by whom, and with whom, and in whom,
in the unity of the Holy Spirit,
all honour and glory be yours, almighty Father,
for ever and ever.
Amen.

Hymn Christ is made the sure foundation (v 4)

13 *The Lord's Prayer*

As our Saviour taught us, so we pray

**Our Father in heaven,
hallowed be your name,
your kingdom come,
your will be done,
on earth as in heaven.
Give us today our daily bread.
Forgive us our sins
as we forgive those who sin against us.
Lead us not into temptation
but deliver us from evil.
For the kingdom, the power, and the glory are yours
now and for ever.
Amen.**

14 *Breaking of the Bread*

The president breaks the consecrated bread.

We break this bread
to share in the body of Christ.
**Though we are many, we are one body,
because we all share in one bread.**

15 *Giving of Communion*

The president says the invitation to Communion

Jesus is the Lamb of God
who takes away the sin of the world.
Blessed are those who are called to his supper.
**Lord, I am not worthy to receive you,
but only say the word, and I shall be healed.**

Towards the end of the Eucharistic Prayer the background music leads into a clear and bold introduction to the final verse of Christ is made the sure foundation.

Music ends.

**We do not presume
to come to this your table, merciful Lord,
trusting in our own righteousness,
but in your manifold and great mercies.
We are not worthy
so much as to gather up the crumbs
under your table.
But you are the same Lord
whose nature is always to have mercy.
Grant us therefore, gracious Lord,
so to eat the flesh of your dear Son Jesus Christ
and to drink his blood,
that our sinful bodies may be made clean
by his body
and our souls washed
through his most precious blood,
and that we may evermore dwell in him
and he in us.
Amen.**

The president and people receive Communion.

During communion the worship band or music group play instrumental versions of several songs.

Silence

Music ends.

16 *Prayer after Communion*

God of all mercy,
in this eucharist you have set aside our sins
and given us your healing:
grant that we who are made whole in Christ
may bring that healing to this broken world,
in the name of Jesus Christ our Lord.

**We thank you, Lord,
that you have fed us in this sacrament,
united us with Christ,
and given us a foretaste of the heavenly banquet
prepared for all peoples.
Amen.**

Following the prayer the song 'Could I bring you words of comfort' is announced.

Songs Could I bring you words of comfort (*The Source 2*)
He is the Lord (*The Source*)

17 *Blessing*

Before the Blessing and Dismissal offer the opportunity for prayer ministry.

The peace of God,
which passes all understanding,
keep your hearts and minds
in the knowledge and love of God,
and of his Son Jesus Christ our Lord;
and the blessing of God almighty,
the Father, the Son, and the Holy Spirit,
be among you and remain with you always.
Amen.

Go in peace to love and serve the Lord.
In the name of Christ. Amen.

Song The Grace (*The Source 2*)

18 *Prayer Ministry Available*

The Grace is sung to one another.

Soft worship music could be played or
sung as people leave or as prayer continues.

Fifteenth Sunday after Trinity
Service of the Word with Holy Communion

Order of Service

1 The Gathering

As people enter church and as they wait for the start of the worship, images of the world could be projected onto a screen. These could include pictures of creation, nature and people of the world. Appropriate background music could accompany the images.

2 Welcome and Introduction

Stand

3 Extended time of sung worship

Songs You are a holy God (*The Source 2*)
Joy to the world (*The Source*)
Be still, for the presence of the Lord (*The Source*)

4 Open Worship

(Open to God, open prayer or praise, reflecting, sharing gifts of the Spirit)

Sit if not already doing so.

Ministry Song Father, to you (*The Source 2*) (Sung to the congregation)

5 Confession

Let us return to the Lord our God and say to him:

Father,
we have sinned against heaven and against you.
We are not worthy to be called your children.
We turn to you again.
Have mercy on us,
bring us back to yourself
as those who once were dead
but now have life through Christ our Lord. Amen.

The president says

May the God of love
bring *us* back to himself,
forgive *us our* sins,
and assure *us* of his eternal love
in Jesus Christ our Lord.
Amen.

Directions

Warm and inviting. Visitors and newcomers should be made particularly welcome. A clear verbal outline of the service could be given.

The first song is announced.

'Be still' should be sung with strength at a majestic pace.

Sensitive instrumental music continues in the background. Open to the Holy Spirit. It may be appropriate to encourage the congregation to be free in their expression of worship at this point (e.g. to speak out prayer or to pray silently). It is important for the worship leader to direct worship sensitively at this point.

The Ministry Song follows any open worship at an appropriate moment. An accompanying image could be projected onto a screen during the song, e.g. a child holding their father's hand.

Gentle background music continues during the Confession and Absolution.

Silence

6 *The Collect*

God, who in generous mercy sent the Holy Spirit
upon your Church in the burning fire of your love:
grant that your people may be fervent
in the fellowship of the gospel
that, always abiding in you,
they may be found steadfast in faith
and active in service;
through Jesus Christ your Son our Lord.
Amen

7 *The Peace*

Invite the congregation to stand.

Blessed are the peacemakers:
they shall be called children of God.
We meet in the name of Christ and share his peace.

The peace of the Lord be always with you
and also with you.

Let us offer one another a sign of peace.

All may exchange a sign of peace.

8 *The Liturgy of the Word*
First Reading

Silence

(Second Reading)

Silence

Sermon
Less formal exposition. Drama, interviews, testimonies,
discussion, stories, illustrations or audio-visuals could be
used within the Sermon or in between parts of the Sermon.

Silence

Stand
Song Sing a song for the nations (*The Source 2*)

9 *Affirmation of Faith*

Let us declare our faith in God:

**We believe in God the Father,
from whom every family
in heaven and on earth is named.**

**We believe in God the Son,
who lives in our hearts through faith,
and fills us with his love.**

**We believe in God the Holy Spirit,
who strengthens us
with power from on high.**

After the Absolution the background music ends.

The reading follows unannounced.

Sermon linked to the overall theme if there is one. Challenging and affirming, giving practical help for discipleship. Contemporary and relevant, linking with everyday life.

Silence used to reflect on the Sermon.

The song is announced.

During the Affirmation of Faith a musical introduction for the approaching song starts and builds in strength.

We believe in one God;
Father, Son and Holy Spirit. Amen.

Song We have a vision (*The Source 2*)

The song follows the Affirmation of Faith unannounced.

Music ends.

10 *Prayers of Intercession*

(Visual open prayer)
Projected images and headings are used as prayer guides. Space is given for open prayer in which people are free to pray their own prayers either silently or aloud. Contemporary, atmospheric background music (played live or from a recording) accompanies the time of prayer.

The prayers may follow this sequence:

- The Church of Christ
- Creation, human society, the Sovereign and those in authority
- The local community
- Those who suffer
- The communion of saints

At the end of the prayers the service leader could introduce the following response:

Merciful Father,
accept these prayers
for the sake of your Son,
our Saviour Jesus Christ.
Amen.

During the concluding response the introduction to 'Sing a song for the nations' begins.

Song Sing a song for the nations (chorus)

The song then follows the prayers unannounced.

Music ends.

11 *Eucharistic Prayer (H)*

The Lord be with you
and also with you.

Lift up your hearts.
We lift them to the Lord.

Let us give thanks to the Lord our God.
It is right to give thanks and praise.

It is right to praise you, Father, Lord of all creation;
in your love you made us for yourself.

When we turned away
you did not reject us,
but came to meet us in your Son.
You embraced us as your children
and welcomed us to sit and eat with you.

In Christ you shared our life
that we might live in him and he in us.
He opened his arms of love upon the cross
and made for all the perfect sacrifice for sin.

On the night he was betrayed,
at supper with his friends
he took bread, and gave you thanks;

he broke it and gave it to them, saying:
Take, eat; this is my body which is given for you;
do this in remembrance of me.
Father, we do this in remembrance of him:
his body is the bread of life.

At the end of supper, taking the cup of wine,
he gave you thanks, and said:
Drink this, all of you;
this is my blood of the new covenant,
which is shed for you for the forgiveness of sins;
do this in remembrance of me.
Father, we do this in remembrance of him:
his blood is shed for all.

As we proclaim his death
and celebrate his rising in glory,
send your Holy Spirit that this bread and this wine
may be to us the body and blood of your dear Son.

As we eat and drink these holy gifts
make us one in Christ, our risen Lord.

With your whole Church throughout the world
we offer you this sacrifice of praise
and lift our voice to join the eternal song of heaven:

Holy, holy, holy Lord,
God of power and might,
Heaven and earth are full of your glory.
Hosanna in the highest.

12 *The Lord's Prayer*

As our Saviour taught us, so we pray

Our Father in heaven,
hallowed be your name,
your kingdom come,
your will be done,
on earth as in heaven.
Give us today our daily bread.
Forgive us our sins
as we forgive those who sin against us.
Lead us not into temptation
but deliver us from evil.
For the kingdom, the power, and the glory are yours
now and for ever.
Amen.

13 *Breaking of the Bread*

The president breaks the consecrated bread.

We break this bread
to share in the body of Christ.
Though we are many, we are one body,
because we all share in one bread.

14 *Giving of Communion and Prayer Ministry*

The president says the invitation to Communion

God's holy gifts
for God's holy people.
Jesus Christ is holy,
Jesus Christ is Lord,
to the glory of God the Father.

We do not presume
to come to this your table, merciful Lord,
trusting in our own righteousness,
but in your manifold and great mercies.
We are not worthy
so much as to gather up the crumbs
under your table.
But you are the same Lord
whose nature is always to have mercy.
Grant us therefore, gracious Lord,
so to eat the flesh of your dear Son Jesus Christ
and to drink his blood,
that our sinful bodies
may be made clean by his body
and our souls washed
through his most precious blood,
and that we may evermore dwell in him
and he in us.
Amen.

The president and people receive Communion and/or prayer ministry.

(During Communion prayer ministry is also offered. The prayer ministry team should be situated in an appropriate area of church where the congregation may receive prayer after receiving communion. Worship songs are sung.)

Songs All of heaven's treasure (*Release*)
Jesus, be the centre (*The Source 2*)
One name (*The Source 2*)

Silence

Music ends.

15 *Prayer after Communion*

Father of all,
we give you thanks and praise,
that when we were still far off
you met us in your Son and brought us home.
Dying and living, he declared your love,
gave us grace, and opened the gate of glory.
May we who share Christ's body live his risen life;
we who drink his cup bring life to others;
we whom the Spirit lights give light to the world.
Keep us firm in the hope you have set before us,
so we and all your children shall be free,
and the whole earth live to praise your name;
through Christ our Lord.
Amen.

Hymn O for a thousand tongues to sing (*The Source*)

The hymn is announced.

Before the Commissioning and Blessing offer the additional opportunity for prayer ministry.

16 *Commissioning and Blessing*

Go forth into the world in peace;
be of good courage;
hold fast to that which is good;
render to no one evil for evil;
strengthen the faint hearted; support the weak;
help the afflicted; honour everyone;
love and serve the Lord,
rejoicing in the power of the Spirit.
And the blessing of God almighty,
the Father, the Son, and the Holy Spirit,
be among you and remain with you always.
Amen.

17 *Prayer Ministry Available*

Soft worship music could be played or sung as people leave or as prayer continues.

Eighteenth Sunday after Trinity
Service of the Word

Order of Service

<table>
<tr><td></td><td></td></tr>
</table>

Order of Service

1 **Welcome and Introduction**

Stand

2 **Opening Prayer**

The service/worship leader opens with prayer

3 **Extended Time of Sung Worship**

Songs Come, now is the time to worship (*The Source 2*)
Should he who made the stars (*The Source 2*)
All I want is to know you, Jesus (*The Source 2*)

4 **Open Worship**

(Open to God, open prayer or praise, reflecting, sharing gifts of the Spirit)

Sit if not already doing so.

5 **Invitation to Confession**

Humbled before the majesty of the Lord
we see ourselves in a true light.
We give to God the things that burden our hearts,
things we should not have done
and things we have failed to do.

Silence

God be gracious to us and bless us,
and make your face shine upon us:
Lord, have mercy.
Lord, have mercy.

May your ways be known on the earth,
your saving power among the nations:
Christ, have mercy.
Christ, have mercy.

You, Lord, have made known your salvation,
and reveal your justice in the sight of the nations:
Lord, have mercy.
Lord, have mercy.

The president says

May almighty God,
who sent his Son into the world to save sinners,
bring *you* his pardon and peace,
now and for ever.
Amen.

Directions

Warm and inviting. Visitors and newcomers should be made particularly welcome. A clear verbal outline of the service could be given.

The first song is announced.

Sensitive instrumental music continues in the background. Open to the Holy Spirit. It may be appropriate to encourage the congregation to be free in their expression of worship at this point (e.g. to speak out prayer or to pray silently). It is important for the worship leader to direct worship sensitively at this point.

The Prayers of Penitence follow any open worship at an appropriate moment. Music ends.

6 *Verses of Scripture*

(Ephesians 2:4-10)

Hymn *May the mind of Christ my Saviour (The Source 2)*

Silence

7 *The Collect*

> Almighty and everlasting God,
> increase in us your gift of faith
> that, forsaking what lies behind
> and reaching out to that which is before,
> we may run the way of your commandments
> and win the crown of everlasting joy;
> through Jesus Christ your Son our Lord,
> who is alive and reigns with you,
> in the unity of the Holy Spirit,
> one God, now and for ever.
> **Amen**

Ministry song Lord, you've been good to me *(The Source 2)*
Performed live or played from CD *(What Grace* – Graham
Kendrick) to the congregation.
(Images to accompany the song could be projected onto
the screen. Mime or dance could be performed.)

8 *The Liturgy of the Word*
First Reading

Silence

Talk
Less formal exposition. Drama, interviews, testimonies,
discussion, stories, illustrations or audio-visuals could be
used within the Talk or in between parts of the Talk.

Silence

Stand

9 *Affirmation of Faith*

> Let us declare our faith in God:

> **We believe in God the Father,**
> **from whom every family**
> **in heaven and on earth is named.**

> **We believe in God the Son,**
> **who lives in our hearts through faith,**
> **and fills us with his love.**

> **We believe in God the Holy Spirit,**
> **who strengthens us**
> **with power from on high.**

> **We believe in one God;**
> **Father, Son and Holy Spirit.**
> **Amen.**

During the verses of scripture a musical introduction to the approaching hymn begins.

The music ends.

The ministry song begins immediately after the Collect.

The reading follows unannounced.

Talk linked to the overall theme if there is one. Challenging and affirming, giving practical help for discipleship. Contemporary and relevant, linking with everyday life.

Silence used to reflect on the Talk.

10 *Prayers of Intercession*

One person may lead the prayers verbally but other more creative forms of prayer could be used, e.g. visual prayer using projected images as prayer guides, group prayer or open prayer in which people are free to pray their own prayers either silently or aloud. Alternatively, intercessory worship could be used, in which songs provide the framework for open prayer, guided by the worship or service leader. Prophecies and other spiritual gifts could be expressed. Artwork, dance, signing and contemporary/classical background music could also be used creatively within this section of the service.

The prayers may follow this sequence:
- The Church of Christ
- Creation, human society, the Sovereign and those in authority
- The local community
- Those who suffer
- The communion of saints

The following response may be used to conclude sections of prayer:

Lord, in your mercy
hear our prayer.

And at the end of the prayers:

11 *The Lord's Prayer*

As our Saviour taught us, so we pray

**Our Father in heaven,
hallowed be your name,
your kingdom come,
your will be done,
on earth as in heaven.
Give us today our daily bread.
Forgive us our sins
as we forgive those who sin against us.
Lead us not into temptation
but deliver us from evil.
For the kingdom, the power,
and the glory are yours
now and for ever.
Amen.**

12 *Prayer Ministry and Sung Worship*

An extended time of sung worship provides the opportunity for the congregation to respond following the Liturgy of the Word and Intercessions. The worship also provides the environment and backdrop for prayer ministry. Members of the prayer ministry team will need to be on hand in an appropriate area of the church to provide the prayer ministry. The service leader will have to lead sensitively at this point encouraging and inviting the congregation to receive prayer. Some guidance may need to be given as to what they receive prayer for, e.g. 'Come forward to receive prayer if you would like the Lord to increase your heart for evangelism'. Ideas for this guidance may arise naturally from the Liturgy of the Word or Intercessions. Alternatively the service leader may discern a general focus for the prayer ministry by sensing the Holy Spirit at work in a particular way. Members of the congregation would be free to respond to the general focus for prayer or to request prayer for more personal needs.

Suggested songs
Saviour I will sing to you (*Release*)
Your eye is on the sparrow (*The Source 2*)
I will come to you (*The Source 2*)
Jesus, Jesus (*The Source*)

Should he who made the stars (chorus only) (*The Source 2*)

Silence

13 *Conclusion*

At an appropriate moment it will be necessary for the service leader to draw the time of prayer ministry and worship to a close. Some members of the congregation may still be receiving prayer but it is important for the service to finish properly. The leader may wish to sum things up briefly or to say a concluding prayer.

14 *Blessing*

Christ the good shepherd,
who laid down his life for the sheep,
draw you and all who hear his voice,
to be one flock within one fold;
and the blessing of God almighty,
the Father, the Son, and the Holy Spirit,
be among you and remain with you always.
Amen.

15 *Prayer Ministry Available*

Songs linked by extended sections of instrumental music.

'Should he who made the stars' is sung to conclude the time of ministry and worship.

Music ends.

Before the Blessing and Dismissal offer the additional opportunity for prayer ministry following the service.

Soft worship music could be played or sung as people leave or as prayer continues.

Last Sunday after Trinity
Service of Holy Communion

Order of Service

Directions

1 The Gathering

As people enter church and as they wait for the start of worship, the following Bible verses could be projected onto a screen.

'Is not my word like fire,' declares the Lord.
(Jeremiah 23:29)

Your word is a lamp to my feet and a light for my path.
(Psalm 119:105)

If possible, an appropriate image could be displayed in the background to each verse, e.g. flames for Jeremiah 23:29 and light or a lamp for Psalm 119:105. Subtle music could be played during the gathering.

Stand

Hymn O God beyond all praising
        (*Complete Anglican Hymns Old & New*)

The opening hymn is announced.

Sit

2 Welcome and Introduction

Warm and inviting. Visitors and newcomers should be made particularly welcome. A clear verbal outline of the service could be given.

3 Prayer of Preparation

**Almighty God,
to whom all hearts are open,
all desires known,
and from whom no secrets are hidden:
cleanse the thoughts of our hearts
by the inspiration of your Holy Spirit,
that we may perfectly love you,
and worthily magnify your holy name;
through Christ our Lord.
Amen.**

4 Extended Time of Sung Worship

Songs All people that on earth do dwell (*The Source*)
        Love divine, all loves excelling (*The Source*)

5 Open worship

(Open to God, open prayer or praise, reflecting, sharing gifts of the Spirit)

Sensitive instrumental music continues in the background. Open to the Holy Spirit. It may be appropriate to encourage the congregation to be free in their expression of worship at this point (e.g. to speak out prayer/thanksgiving or to pray silently). It is important for the worship leader to direct worship sensitively at this point.

Sit if not already doing so.

6 *Prayers of Penitence*

The Summary of the Law

Our Lord Jesus Christ said:
The first commandment is this:
'Hear, O Israel, the Lord our God is the only Lord.
You shall love the Lord your God with all your heart,
with all your soul, with all your mind,
and with all your strength.'

The second is this: 'Love your neighbour as yourself.'
There is no other commandment greater than these.
On these two commandments hang all the law and the
prophets.

Amen. Lord, have mercy.

7 *Invitation to Confession*

Silence

(During the time of silence the following verse could be
projected onto a screen for the congregation to meditate
on.)

*For the word of God is living and active. Sharper than any
double-edged sword, it penetrates even to dividing soul and
spirit, joints and marrow; it judges the thoughts and attitudes
of the heart.* (Hebrews 4:12)

May your loving mercy come to me, O Lord,
and your salvation according to your word:
Lord, have mercy.
Lord, have mercy.

Your word is a lantern to my feet and a light to my path:
Christ, have mercy.
Christ, have mercy.

O let your mercy come to me that I may live,
for your law is my delight:
Lord, have mercy.
Lord, have mercy.

The president says

Almighty God,
who in Jesus Christ has given us
a kingdom that cannot be destroyed,
forgive *us our* sins,
open *our* eyes to God's truth,
strengthen *us* to do God's will
and give *us* the joy of his kingdom,
through Jesus Christ our Lord.
Amen.

Silence

8 *The Collect*

Blessed Lord,
who caused all holy Scriptures to be written for our
learning:

Gentle background music continues during
the Summary of the Law.

Music ends.

help us so to hear them,
to read, mark, learn and inwardly digest them
that, through patience,
and the comfort of your holy word,
we may embrace and for ever hold fast
the hope of everlasting life,
which you have given us in our Saviour Jesus Christ.
Amen.

9 *The Liturgy of the Word*
First Reading

Silence

Gospel Reading
Stand

Alleluia, alleluia.
Speak, Lord, for your servant is listening.
You have the words of eternal life.
Alleluia.

When the Gospel is announced the reader says

Hear the Gospel of our Lord Jesus Christ according to *N.*
Glory to you, O Lord.

Following the gospel reading

This is the Gospel of the Lord.
Praise to you, O Christ.

Silence following the reading

Sermon
Less formal exposition. Drama, interviews, testimonies,
discussion, stories, illustrations or audio-visuals could be
used within the Sermon or in between parts of the Sermon.

Silence

Stand

10 *The Nicene Creed*

**We believe in one God,
the Father, the Almighty,
maker of heaven and earth,
of all that is, seen and unseen.**

**We believe in one Lord, Jesus Christ,
the only Son of God,
eternally begotten of the Father,
God from God, Light from Light,
true God from true God,
begotten, not made,
of one Being with the Father;
through him all things were made.
For us and for our salvation
he came down from heaven,
was incarnate from the Holy Spirit
and the Virgin Mary
and was made man.**

The reading follows unannounced.

Sermon linked to the overall theme if there
is one. Challenging and affirming, giving
practical help for discipleship. Contemporary
and relevant, linking with everyday life.

Silence used to reflect on the sermon.

For our sake he was crucified under Pontius Pilate;
he suffered death and was buried.
On the third day he rose again
in accordance with the Scriptures;
he ascended into heaven
and is seated at the right hand of the Father.
He will come again in glory
to judge the living and the dead,
and his kingdom will have no end.

We believe in the Holy Spirit,
the Lord, the giver of life,
who proceeds from the Father and the Son,
who with the Father and the Son
is worshipped and glorified,
who has spoken through the prophets.
We believe in one holy catholic and apostolic Church.
We acknowledge one baptism
for the forgiveness of sins.
We look for the resurrection of the dead,
and the life of the world to come.
Amen.

Song O Lord, hear my prayer (*The Source*)

11 *Intercessory Worship*

Sung worship providing the framework for or leading into open prayer (prayers offered by the congregation either silently or aloud)

'O Lord, hear my prayer' is used as a refrain during the intercessions. It could be used to conclude each section of prayer. Prayers could be directed by headings projected onto a screen. Alternatively, a prayer leader could say spontaneous or written prayers whilst leaving space for open prayer. In some churches this form of prayer may lead to the sharing of prophecies and other spiritual gifts. Some gifted musicians or members of the congregation may be able to sing prayers, prophecies or passages of scripture. This could be facilitated during this section of worship. Projected images, artwork, dance and signing could also be used creatively within this section of the service.

Song O Lord, hear my prayer (*The Source*)

• Prayer for the Church

Song O Lord, hear my prayer (*The Source*)

• Prayer for the world, leaders and our nation

Song O Lord, hear my prayer (*The Source*)

• Prayer for your local community

Song O Lord, hear my prayer (*The Source*)

• Prayer for the suffering and those in need

Song O Lord, hear my prayer (*The Source*)

12 *The Liturgy of the Sacrament*

The Peace

Invite the congregation to stand.

Music ends.

God is love
and those who live in love live in God
and God lives in them.

The peace of the Lord be always with you
and also with you.

Let us offer one another a sign of peace.

All may exchange a sign of peace.

Hymn Lord, enthroned in heavenly splendour (vv 1-4)
(*The Source 2*)

The hymn is announced.

13 *Eucharistic Prayer (B)*

The Lord be with you
and also with you.

Lift up your hearts.
We lift them to the Lord.

Let us give thanks to the Lord our God.
It is right to give thanks and praise.

It is truly right and just, our duty and our salvation,
always and everywhere to give you thanks,
holy Father, almighty and eternal God.
From sunrise to sunset this day is holy,
for Christ has risen from the tomb
and scattered the darkness of death
with light that will not fade.
This day the risen Lord walks with your gathered people,
unfolds for us your word,
and makes himself known in the breaking of the bread.
And though the night will overtake this day
you summon us to live in endless light,
the never-ceasing sabbath of the Lord.
And so, with choirs of angels
and with all the heavenly host,
we proclaim your glory
and join their unending song of praise:

Holy, holy, holy Lord,
God of power and might,
heaven and earth are full of your glory.
Hosanna in the highest.

Lord, you are holy indeed, the source of all holiness;
grant that by the power of your Holy Spirit,
and according to your holy will,
these gifts of bread and wine
may be to us the body and blood of our Lord Jesus Christ;

who, in the same night that he was betrayed,
took bread and gave you thanks;
he broke it and gave it to his disciples, saying:
Take, eat; this is my body which is given for you;
do this in remembrance of me.

In the same way, after supper
he took the cup and gave you thanks;
he gave it to them, saying:

Instrumental music of the hymn continues
softly during the Eucharistic Prayer.

Drink this, all of you;
this is my blood of the new covenant,
which is shed for you and for many
for the forgiveness of sins.
Do this, as often as you drink it,
in remembrance of me.

Hymn Lord, enthroned in heavenly splendour (v 5)
     (*The Source 2*)

And so, Father, calling to mind his death on the cross,
his perfect sacrifice made once
for the sins of the whole world;
rejoicing in his mighty resurrection and glorious ascension,
and looking for his coming in glory,
we celebrate this memorial of our redemption.
As we offer you this our sacrifice
of praise and thanksgiving,
we bring before you this bread and this cup
and we thank you for counting us worthy
to stand in your presence and serve you.

Send the Holy Spirit on your people
and gather into one in your kingdom
all who share this one bread and one cup,
so that we, in the company of [*N and*] all the saints,
may praise and glorify you for ever,
through Jesus Christ our Lord;

by whom, and with whom, and in whom,
in the unity of the Holy Spirit,
all honour and glory be yours, almighty Father,
for ever and ever.
Amen.

14 *The Lord's Prayer*

As our Saviour taught us, so we pray

Our Father in heaven,
hallowed be your name,
your kingdom come,
your will be done,
on earth as in heaven.
Give us today our daily bread.
Forgive us our sins
as we forgive those who sin against us.
Lead us not into temptation
but deliver us from evil.
For the kingdom, the power, and the glory are yours
now and for ever.
Amen.

15 *Breaking of the Bread*

The president breaks the consecrated bread.

We break this bread
to share in the body of Christ.
Though we are many, we are one body,
because we all share in one bread.

The instrumental music grows into a clear and bold introduction to the final verse of the hymn.

Music ends.

16 *Giving of Communion and Prayer Ministry*

The president says the invitation to Communion

God's holy gifts
for God's holy people.
**Jesus Christ is holy,
Jesus Christ is Lord,
to the glory of God the Father.**

**We do not presume
to come to this your table, merciful Lord,
trusting in our own righteousness,
but in your manifold and great mercies.
We are not worthy
so much as to gather up the crumbs
under your table.
But you are the same Lord
whose nature is always to have mercy.
Grant us therefore, gracious Lord,
so to eat the flesh of your dear Son Jesus Christ
and to drink his blood,
that our sinful bodies may be made clean
by his body
and our souls washed
through his most precious blood,
and that we may evermore dwell in him
and he in us.
Amen.**

The president and people receive communion and/or prayer ministry.

(During communion prayer ministry is also offered. The prayer ministry team should be situated in an appropriate area of church where the congregation may receive prayer after receiving communion. Appropriate background music could be played by the organist or music group.)

Silence

17 *Prayer after Communion*

God of all grace,
your Son Jesus Christ fed the hungry
with the bread of his life
and the word of his kingdom:
renew your people with your heavenly grace,
and in all our weakness
sustain us by your true and living bread;
who is alive and reigns, now and for ever.

**You have opened to us the Scriptures, O Christ,
and you have made yourself known
in the breaking of the bread.
Abide with us, we pray,
that, blessed by your royal presence,
we may walk with you
all the days of our life,
and at its end behold you**

**in the glory of the eternal Trinity,
one God for ever and ever.
Amen.**

18 *Blessing*

Christ, who has nourished us with himself the living bread,
make you one in praise and love,
and raise you up at the last day;
and the blessing of God almighty,
the Father, the Son, and the Holy Spirit,
be among you and remain with you always.
Amen.

Hymn From all that dwell below the skies (*The Bridge*)

Go in peace to love and serve the Lord.
In the name of Christ. Amen.

Song The Grace (*The Source 2*)

19 *Prayer Ministry Available*

Before the Dismissal offer the additional opportunity for prayer ministry.

The Grace is sung to one another.

Soft worship music could be played or sung as people leave or as prayer continues.

Fourth Sunday before Advent
Service of Holy Communion

Order of Service

1 The Gathering

Worship songs reflecting a call to worship/desire for God/the nature of God to be played as people enter or as refreshments are served before the service. People should be free to greet each other, sit quietly or join in with the songs.

Song suggestions for a call to worship:
Father of creation (*The Source*)
Clothed with splendour and majesty (*The Source 2*)
I have come to love you (*The Source*)

2 Welcome and Introduction

Stand

3 Prayer of Preparation

> **Almighty God,**
> **to whom all hearts are open,**
> **all desires known,**
> **and from whom no secrets are hidden:**
> **cleanse the thoughts of our hearts**
> **by the inspiration of your Holy Spirit,**
> **that we may perfectly love you,**
> **and worthily magnify your holy name;**
> **through Christ our Lord.**
> **Amen.**

4 Extended Time of Sung Worship including Confession

Songs I will praise you (*Release*)
We have come to a holy mountain (*The Source 2*)

(Invite those present to reflect on their need of forgiveness but also on the overwhelming love God has for them.)

Praise be to the God and Father of our Lord Jesus Christ, who has blessed us in the heavenly realms with every Spiritual blessing in Christ. . . . In him we have redemption through his blood, the forgiveness of sins, in accordance with the riches of God's grace that he lavished on us with all wisdom and understanding. (Ephesians 1:3, 7, 8)

Directions

Songs led by worship band or music group.

Warm and inviting. Visitors and newcomers should be made particularly welcome. A clear verbal outline of the service could be given.

SHORT PAUSE

An introduction to the first song begins immediately after the Prayer of Preparation.

Soft instrumental music continues in the background to Confession.

The passage of scripture could be read or projected onto a screen.

Come, let us return to the Lord and say:

**Lord our God,
in our sin we have avoided your call.
Our love for you is like a morning cloud,
like the dew that goes away early.
Have mercy on us;
deliver us from judgement;
bind up our wounds and revive us;
in Jesus Christ our Lord. Amen.**

May God our Father forgive *us our* sins,
and bring *us* to the fellowship of his table
with his saints for ever.
Amen.

Song Lord, we long to see your glory (*The Source*)

5 *Open Worship*

(Open to God, open prayer or praise, reflecting, sharing
gifts of the Spirit)

Silence

6 *The Collect*

Almighty and eternal God,
you have kindled the flame of love
in the hearts of the saints:
grant to us the same faith and power of love,
that, as we rejoice in their triumphs,
we may be sustained
by their example and fellowship;
through Jesus Christ your Son our Lord,
who is alive and reigns with you,
in the unity of the Holy Spirit,
one God, now and for ever.
Amen.

7 *The Liturgy of the Word*
First Reading

Silence

Gospel Reading
Alleluia, alleluia.
Blessed is the king who comes in the name of the Lord.
Peace in heaven and glory in the highest heaven.
Alleluia.

When the Gospel is announced the reader says

Hear the Gospel of our Lord Jesus Christ according to N.
Glory to you, O Lord.

Background music develops into an
introduction to the next song.

Sensitive instrumental music continues in
the background. Open to the Holy Spirit.
It may be appropriate to encourage the
congregation to be free in their expression
of worship at this point (e.g. to speak out
prayer or to pray silently). It is important
for the worship leader to direct worship
sensitively at this point.

Music ends.

The reading follows unannounced.

Following the Gospel reading

> This is the Gospel of the Lord.
> **Praise to you, O Christ.**

Silence following the reading

Sermon
Less formal exposition. Drama, interviews, testimonies, discussion, stories, illustrations or audio-visuals could be used within the Sermon or in between parts of the Sermon.

Silence

Ministry Song Nothing compares (*Release*)
(Sung to the congregation. Images to accompany the song could be projected onto the screen. Mime or dance could be performed.)

Stand

8 **The Nicene Creed**

> **We believe in one God,**
> **the Father, the Almighty,**
> **maker of heaven and earth,**
> **of all that is,**
> **seen and unseen.**
>
> **We believe in one Lord, Jesus Christ,**
> **the only Son of God,**
> **eternally begotten of the Father,**
> **God from God, Light from Light,**
> **true God from true God,**
> **begotten, not made,**
> **of one Being with the Father;**
> **through him all things were made.**
> **For us and for our salvation**
> **he came down from heaven,**
> **was incarnate from the Holy Spirit**
> **and the Virgin Mary**
> **and was made man.**
> **For our sake he was crucified under Pontius Pilate;**
> **he suffered death and was buried.**
> **On the third day he rose again**
> **in accordance with the Scriptures;**
> **he ascended into heaven**
> **and is seated at the right hand of the Father.**
> **He will come again in glory**
> **to judge the living and the dead,**
> **and his kingdom will have no end.**
>
> **We believe in the Holy Spirit,**
> **the Lord, the giver of life,**
> **who proceeds from the Father and the Son,**
> **who with the Father and the Son**
> **is worshipped and glorified,**
> **who has spoken through the prophets.**
> **We believe in one holy catholic and apostolic Church.**
> **We acknowledge one baptism**
> **for the forgiveness of sins.**

Sermon linked to the overall theme if there is one. Challenging and affirming, giving practical help for discipleship. Contemporary and relevant, linking with everyday life.

Silence used to reflect on the Sermon.

Performed as a solo or by the whole music group.

**We look for the resurrection of the dead,
and the life of the world to come.
Amen.**

9 *Prayers of Intercession*

One person may lead the prayers verbally but other more creative forms of prayer could be used, e.g. visual prayer using projected images or headings as prayer guides, group prayer or open prayer (in which people are free to pray their own prayers either silently or aloud). Alternatively, intercessory worship could be used in which songs provide the framework for open prayer, guided by the worship or service leader. Prophecies and other spiritual gifts could be expressed. Dance, mime and other artwork can also be incorporated.

The prayers may follow this sequence:
• The Church of Christ
• Creation, human society, the Sovereign and those in authority
• The local community
• Those who suffer
• The communion of saints

The following response may be used to conclude sections of prayer:

Lord, in your mercy
hear our prayer.

And at the end of the prayers:

Merciful Father,
**accept these prayers
for the sake of your Son,
our Saviour Jesus Christ.
Amen.**

10 *The Liturgy of the Sacrament*

The Peace

Invite the congregation to stand.

To crown all things there must be love,
to bind all together and complete the whole.
Let the peace of Christ rule in our hearts.

The peace of the Lord be always with you
and also with you.

Let us offer one another a sign of peace.

All may exchange a sign of peace.

Song Say the name of love (*The Source 2*)

11 *Eucharistic Prayer (E)*

The Lord be with you
and also with you.

During the Peace an extended musical introduction to the song is played. The song starts as people have returned to their places.

Instrumental music of the song continues gently in the background to the Eucharistic Prayer.

Lift up your hearts.
We lift them to the Lord.

Let us give thanks to the Lord our God.
It is right to give thanks and praise.

Father, you made the world and love your creation.
You gave your Son Jesus Christ to be our Saviour.
His dying and rising have set us free
from sin and death.
And so we gladly thank you,
with saints and angels praising you, and saying:

Holy, holy, holy Lord,
God of power and might,
heaven and earth are full of your glory.
Hosanna in the highest.
[Blessed is he who comes in the name of the Lord.
Hosanna in the highest.]

We praise and bless you, loving Father,
through Jesus Christ, our Lord;
and as we obey his command,
send your Holy Spirit,
that broken bread and wine outpoured
may be for us the body and blood of your dear Son.

On the night before he died
he had supper with his friends
and, taking bread, he praised you.
He broke the bread, gave it to them and said:
Take, eat; this is my body which is given for you;
do this in remembrance of me.

When supper was ended he took the cup of wine.
Again he praised you, gave it to them and said:
Drink this, all of you;
this is my blood of the new covenant,
which is shed for you and for many
for the forgiveness of sins.
Do this, as often as you drink it, in remembrance of me.

So, Father, we remember all that Jesus did,
in him we plead with confidence his sacrifice
made once for all upon the cross.

Bringing before you the bread of life and cup of salvation,
we proclaim his death and resurrection
until he comes in glory.

Christ is the bread of life:
When we eat this bread and drink this cup,
we proclaim your death, Lord Jesus,
until you come in glory.

Lord of all life,
help us to work together for that day
when your kingdom comes
and justice and mercy will be seen in all the earth.

Look with favour on your people,
gather us in your loving arms
and bring us with [N and] all the saints
to feast at your table in heaven.

Through Christ, and with Christ, and in Christ,
in the unity of the Holy Spirit,
all honour and glory are yours, O loving Father,
for ever and ever.
Amen.

Song Say the name of love (chorus) (*The Source 2*)

12 *Breaking of the Bread*

The president breaks the consecrated bread.

Every time we eat this bread
and drink this cup,
**we proclaim the Lord's death
until he comes.**

13 *Giving of Communion and Prayer Ministry*

The president says the invitation to Communion

Jesus is the Lamb of God
who takes away the sin of the world.
Blessed are those who are called to his supper.
**Lord, I am not worthy to receive you,
but only say the word, and I shall be healed.**

**Most merciful Lord,
your love compels us to come in.
Our hands were unclean,
our hearts were unprepared;
we were not fit even to eat the crumbs
from under your table.
But you, Lord, are the God of our salvation,
and share your bread with sinners.
So cleanse and feed us
with the precious body and blood of your Son,
that he may live in us and we in him;
and that we, with the whole company of Christ,
may sit and eat in your kingdom.
Amen.**

The president and people receive Communion.

(During communion prayer ministry is also offered. The prayer ministry team should be situated in an appropriate area of church where the congregation may receive prayer after receiving communion. Appropriate songs/hymns could be sung. Alternatively, instrumental music could be played or silence kept. Recordings of contemporary or classical music could be played.)

Silence

14 *Prayer after Communion*

Lord of heaven,
in this eucharist you have brought us near
to an innumerable company of angels
and to the spirits of the saints made perfect:
as in this food of our earthly pilgrimage

Background music develops into clear introduction to the chorus of the song.

As the prayer is started an extended introduction to the approaching song begins.

we have shared their fellowship,
so may we come to share their joy in heaven;
through Jesus Christ our Lord.

Songs Praise him, you heavens (*The Source 2*)
Our God is an awesome God (*The Source 2*)

**Almighty God,
we thank you for feeding us
with the body and blood of your Son Jesus Christ.
Through him we offer you our souls and bodies
to be a living sacrifice.
Send us out
in the power of your Spirit
to live and work
to your praise and glory.
Amen.**

15 *Blessing*

God the Father,
by whose glory Christ was raised from the dead.
Strengthen you to walk with him in his risen life;
and the blessing of God almighty,
the Father, the Son and the Holy Spirit
be among you and remain with you always.
Amen.

Go in the peace of Christ.
Thanks be to God.

16 *Prayer Ministry Available*

Move directly onto the songs.

Music ends.

Before the Blessing and Dismissal offer
the additional opportunity for prayer
ministry.

Soft worship music could be played or
sung as people leave or as prayer continues.

Third Sunday before Advent
Service of Holy Communion

Order of Service

1 The Gathering

Contemporary worship music CD to be played as people enter or as refreshments are served before the service. People should be free to greet each other or to sit quietly.

2 Welcome and Introduction

3 Prayer of Preparation

The service/worship leader opens in prayer.

Verse of Scripture
Now to the King eternal, immortal, invisible, the only God, be honour and glory for ever and ever. Amen. (1 Timothy 1:17)

4 Extended Time of Sung Worship including Confession and Intercession

Songs You are the Sovereign 'I Am' (*The Source 2*)
Lord we come before your throne (*The Source 2*)
Every knee shall bow (Chorale from 'Here is the risen Son') (*The Source 2*)

5 Open Worship

(Open to God, open prayer or praise, reflecting, sharing gifts of the Spirit)

6 Confession

God is light; in him there is no darkness at all.
If we claim to have fellowship with him
yet walk in the darkness,
we lie and do not live by the truth.
But if we walk in the light, as he is in the light,
we have fellowship with one another,
and the blood of Jesus, his Son, purifies us from all sin.
If we claim to be without sin, we deceive ourselves
and the truth is not in us.
If we confess our sins, he is faithful and just
and will forgive us our sins
and purify us from all unrighteousness. (1 John 1:5-9)

We confess our sins to God.

Directions

Warm and inviting. Visitors and newcomers should be made particularly welcome. A clear verbal outline of the service could be given.

SHORT PAUSE

An introduction to the first song begins immediately after the verse of scripture.

Sensitive instrumental music continues in the background. Open to the Holy Spirit. It may be appropriate to encourage the congregation to be free in their expression of worship at this point (e.g. to speak out prayer or to pray silently). It is important for the worship leader to direct worship sensitively at this point.

Soft instrumental music continues in the background to Confession.

Silence (except for background music)

> May God who loved the world so much
> that he sent his Son to be our Saviour
> forgive *us our* sins
> and make *us* holy to serve him in the world,
> through Jesus Christ our Lord.
> **Amen.**

Hymn O Breath of life (*The Source*)

7 *Intercessory Worship*

A time of open prayer following on from sung worship in which the congregation is free to offer prayers silently or aloud. This may arise naturally from the worship if the church is used to doing things in this way. Otherwise clear guidance will be needed from the service/worship leader. Prayers could be directed by theme headings projected onto a screen. In some churches this form of open prayer may lead to the sharing of prophecies and other spiritual gifts. Some gifted musicians or members of the congregation may be able to sing prayers or prophecies. This could be facilitated during this section of worship. Projected images, artwork, dance and signing could also be used creatively within this section of the service. Verses of the previous hymn could be used as a refrain within this part of the worship. Alternatively, one of the verses could be sung again to conclude this section.

Silence

8 *The Collect*

> Almighty Father,
> whose will is to restore all things
> in your beloved Son, the King of all:
> govern the hearts and minds of those in authority,
> and bring the families of the nations,
> divided and torn apart by the ravages of sin,
> to be subject to his just and gentle rule;
> who is alive and reigns with you,
> in the unity of the Holy Spirit,
> one God, now and for ever.
> **Amen.**

9 *The Liturgy of the Word*

First Reading

Silence

Gospel Reading
> Alleluia, alleluia.
> Blessed is the king who comes in the name of the Lord.
> Peace in heaven and glory in the highest heaven.
> **Alleluia.**

Side notes:

Silence used for private confession.

Instrumental music develops into an introduction to the next hymn.

Soft background music continues.

Music ends.

The reading follows unannounced.

When the Gospel is announced the reader says

Hear the Gospel of our Lord Jesus Christ according to *N*.
Glory to you, O Lord.

Following the Gospel reading

This is the Gospel of the Lord.
Praise to you, O Christ.

Silence following the reading

Sermon
Less formal exposition. Drama, interviews, testimonies,
discussion, stories, illustrations or audio-visuals could be
used within the Sermon or in between parts of the Sermon.

10 *Response and Reflection*

Silence

Taizé chant Wait for the Lord
(*Complete Anglican Hymns Old & New*)

Silence

Taizé chant Wait for the Lord

Silence

Stand

11 *Affirmation of Faith*

Please stand.

Do you believe and trust in God the Father,
source of all being and life,
the one for whom we exist?
We believe and trust in him.

Do you believe and trust in God the Son,
who took our human nature,
died for us and rose again?
We believe and trust in him.

Do you believe and trust in God the Holy Spirit,
who gives life to the people of God
and makes Christ known in the world?
We believe and trust in him.

This is the faith of the Church.
This is our faith.
We believe and trust in one God,
Father, Son and Holy Spirit. Amen.

12 *The Liturgy of the Sacrament*

The Peace

Invite the congregation to stand.

To crown all things there must be love,
to bind all together and complete the whole.
Let the peace of Christ rule in our hearts.

Sermon linked to the overall theme if there
is one. Challenging and affirming, giving
practical help for discipleship. Contemporary
and relevant, linking with everyday life.

Taizé chant could be sung accompanied or
unaccompanied.

The peace of the Lord be always with you
and also with you.

Let us offer one another a sign of peace.

All may exchange a sign of peace.

Song We humbly pray (*Release*)

13 *Eucharistic Prayer (F)*

The Lord be with you
and also with you.

Lift up your hearts.
We lift them to the Lord.

Let us give thanks to the Lord our God.
It is right to give thanks and praise.

You are worthy of our thanks and praise,
Lord God of truth,
for by the breath of your mouth
you have spoken your word,
and all things have come into being.

You fashioned us in your image
and placed us in the garden of your delight.
Though we chose the path of rebellion
you would not abandon your own.

Again and again you drew us into your covenant of grace.
You gave your people the law
and taught us by your prophets
to look for your reign of justice, mercy and peace.

As we watch for the signs of your kingdom on earth,
we echo the song of the angels in heaven,
evermore praising you and saying:

Holy, holy, holy Lord,
God of power and might,
heaven and earth are full of your glory.
Hosanna in the highest.
[Blessed is he who comes in the name of the Lord.
Hosanna in the highest.]

Lord God, you are the most holy one,
enthroned in splendour and light,
yet in the coming of your Son Jesus Christ
you reveal the power of your love
made perfect in our human weakness.

Amen. Lord, we believe.

Embracing our humanity,
Jesus showed us the way of salvation;
loving us to the end,
he gave himself to death for us;
dying for his own,
he set us free from the bonds of sin,
that we might rise and reign with him in glory.

Amen. Lord, we believe.

During the Peace an extended musical introduction to the song is played. The song starts as soon as people have returned to their places.

Instrumental music of the song continues gently in the background to the Eucharistic Prayer.

On the night he gave up himself for us all
he took bread and gave you thanks;
he broke it and gave it to his disciples, saying:
Take, eat; this is my body which is given for you;
do this in remembrance of me.

Amen. Lord, we believe.

In the same way, after supper
he took the cup and gave you thanks;
he gave it to them, saying:
Drink this, all of you;
this is my blood of the new covenant
which is shed for you and for many
for the forgiveness of sins.
Do this, as often as you drink it, in remembrance of me.

Amen. Lord, we believe.

Therefore we proclaim the death
that he suffered on the cross,
we celebrate his resurrection,
his bursting from the tomb,
we rejoice that he reigns at your right hand on high
and we long for his coming in glory.

Amen. Come, Lord Jesus.

As we recall the one, perfect sacrifice of our redemption,
Father, by your Holy Spirit let these gifts of your creation
be to us the body and blood of our Lord Jesus Christ;
form us into the likeness of Christ
and make us a perfect offering in your sight.

Amen. Come, Holy Spirit.

Look with favour on your people
and in your mercy hear the cry of our hearts.
Bless the earth,
heal the sick,
let the oppressed go free
and fill your Church with power from on high.

Amen. Come, Holy Spirit.

Song We humbly pray (v 2 and chorus) (*Release*)

Gather your people from the ends of the earth
to feast with [*N and*] all your saints
at the table in your kingdom,
where the new creation is brought to perfection
in Jesus Christ our Lord;
by whom, and with whom, and in whom,
in the unity of the Holy Spirit,
all honour and glory be yours, almighty Father,
for ever and ever.
Amen.

14 *The Lord's Prayer*

As our Saviour taught us, so we pray

**Our Father in heaven,
hallowed be your name,**

Background music develops into clear introduction to the chorus of the song.

your kingdom come,
your will be done,
on earth as in heaven.
Give us today our daily bread.
Forgive us our sins
as we forgive those who sin against us.
Lead us not into temptation
but deliver us from evil.
For the kingdom, the power, and the glory are yours
now and for ever.
Amen.

15 Breaking of the Bread

The president breaks the consecrated bread.

Every time we eat this bread
and drink this cup,
**we proclaim the Lord's death
until he comes.**

16 Giving of Communion and Prayer Ministry

The president says the invitation to Communion

Draw near with faith.
Receive the body of our Lord Jesus Christ
which he gave for you,
and his blood which he shed for you.
Eat and drink
in remembrance that he died for you,
and feed on him in your hearts
by faith with thanksgiving.

**We do not presume
to come to this your table, merciful Lord,
trusting in our own righteousness,
but in your manifold and great mercies.
We are not worthy
so much as to gather up the crumbs
under your table.
But you are the same Lord
whose nature is always to have mercy.
Grant us therefore, gracious Lord,
so to eat the flesh of your dear Son Jesus Christ
and to drink his blood,
that our sinful bodies may be made clean
by his body
and our souls washed
through his most precious blood,
and that we may evermore dwell in him
and he in us.
Amen.**

The president and people receive Communion.

(During communion prayer ministry is also offered. The prayer ministry team should be situated in an appropriate area of church where the congregation may receive prayer after receiving communion. Appropriate songs/hymns could be sung. Alternatively, instrumental music could be played or silence kept. Recordings of contemporary or classical music could be played.)

Silence

17 *Prayer after Communion*

God of peace,
whose Son Jesus Christ proclaimed the kingdom
and restored the broken to wholeness of life:
look with compassion on the anguish of the world,
and by your healing power
make whole both people and nations;
through our Lord and Saviour Jesus Christ.
Amen.

**Father of all,
we give you thanks and praise,
that when we were still far off
you met us in your Son and brought us home.
Dying and living, he declared your love,
gave us grace, and opened the gate of glory.
May we who share Christ's body live his risen life;
we who drink his cup bring life to others;
we whom the Spirit lights give light to the world.
Keep us firm in the hope you have set before us,
so we and all your children shall be free,
and the whole earth live to praise your name;
through Christ our Lord.
Amen.**

During the prayer an introduction to the approaching hymn begins.

Hymn Crown him with many crowns (*The Source*)
Song Come, let us worship Jesus (v 4, chorus, v 5)
(*The Source*)

Move directly into the hymn following the prayer.
Hymn and song linked with instrumental music.

Before the Blessing offer the additional opportunity for prayer ministry.

18 *Blessing*

Christ our King make you faithful and strong
to do his will,
that you may reign with him in glory;
and the blessing of God almighty,
the Father, the Son, and the Holy Spirit,
be among you and remain with you always.
Amen.

Go in peace to love and serve the Lord.
In the name of Christ. Amen.

19 *Prayer Ministry Available*

Soft worship music could be played or sung as people leave or as prayer continues.

Liquid Worship

Introduction

Liquid Worship is made up by a number of optional zones or stations. Each zone houses a different aspect, part or style of worship (e.g. sung worship, prayer, talk, The Word, Taizé worship). Zones are situated around the main church building and within other church rooms. Members of a congregation are free to move between some or all of the zones as they wish. Each person therefore designs their own shape and flow of worship within the limitations of the options provided. So as to avoid a completely individualistic expression of worship, it is essential that Liquid Worship be topped and tailed with a corporate gathering and expression of worship.

Zones and the ideas contained within them should be fairly simple. Zone preparation and management should be kept to a minimum. It is not essential to have highly gifted people organising zones.

A Liquid Worship service may have an overall theme or follow a theme identified from the Lectionary readings. Zones could explore different aspects of a theme. Alternatively, where there is no overall theme, zones may have their own individual, unrelated themes.

Notes for leaders

- The bigger the premises and the more rooms available, the more options you have for Liquid Worship. However, smaller churches can scale ideas down. Ideally, this type of worship requires a medium-sized church building with three church rooms. With less than three rooms, zones could be cut but if more than three rooms are available zones could be added. Liquid Worship also assumes some flexibility in the use of chancel space and other space within church but not necessarily within the sanctuary.

- The opening gathering should include an introduction to and a brief explanation of Liquid Worship.

- Sung worship should normally take place in the main part of church. For those participating in other zones within church the sung worship becomes background music as it does at other times in our lives, e.g. TV and radio on as background sound and music as we do other things or music played in bars or cafés. This needs explaining to the congregation. We may not be used to background music within church but we are in the rest of our lives.

- A crèche could be provided so that babies and toddlers are cared for whilst parents take part in the worship.

All-age Liquid Worship

The following service outline is designed as an all-age act of Liquid Worship. It is expected that children and parents/guardians visit zones together. Young adults and adults could visit zones alone or in groups. Between zones families or groups could chat about their experiences and thoughts.

The service outline could be governed by one of the following three formats:

Format A (1 hour 15 minutes)

Initial Gathering	10 minutes
Liquid Worship options	50 minutes
Final Gathering (Communion)	15 minutes

Format B (1 hour 15 minutes)

Initial Gathering	10 minutes
Liquid Worship Options	1 hour
Final Gathering	5 minutes

Format C (1 hour)

Initial Gathering	10 minutes
Liquid Worship Options	45 minutes
Final Gathering	5 minutes

Service Outline

This service could have an overall theme or a theme identified from the lectionary readings. Alternatively, each zone could follow its own individual theme.

Initial gathering

Welcome

Introduction to and Explanation of Liquid Worship

Opening Prayer (said by the service leader or a written prayer to be said together)

Opening Hymn or Song

The Initial Dismissal – people sent off to visit the worship zones.

Liquid Worship Options

Zone 1

Sung Worship

Led by music group or worship band in the main part of church. If you are without musicians then the congregation could sing along to CDs. However, the use of CDs would still require someone leading the singing, someone familiar with the flow of the music on the CD.

Voice-overs and spoken directions should be kept to a minimum so as not to distract people participating in other zones within church.

One collection of songs could be used to fill the allocated time or a song cycle lasting 15 or 20 minutes could be repeated two or three times. The collection of songs should follow a flow so that people are led through different aspects of worship.

e.g. Thanksgiving → Praise → Adoration → Intimacy → Desire for God → Commitment

Songs or hymns fitting with each of the above aspects of worship could be selected.

It is important to note that during the service the number of people participating in sung worship will dwindle at times. This will give quite a sparse and empty feel, but this is to be expected.

This zone could also adopt an alternative style of worship such as Iona or Taizé.

Zone 2

The Refreshment Zone

Drinks and a seating area provided. Stools, sofas, chairs or cushions could be set out.

Zone 3

Prayer Zone

In an area within the main church building.

Families or groups could pray together. Alternatively, people may pray alone.

Prayer Option A
Candles and cushions provided for prayer, meditation and contemplation.

Prayer Option B
Visual prayer. A collection of objects, photographs, drawings, magazine/newspaper cuttings or video material could be provided to initiate prayer.

Note: Both prayer options should facilitate confession. Either a written confession printed onto paper or an action confession (e.g. Step 1: Think of the things you have done wrong; hold your sins in clenched fists with the back of your hands facing upwards. Step 2: Ask God to forgive your sins; open your hands and let go of your sin. Step 3: Turn your open hands over so that your palms face upwards and receive God's love). Directions for the action confession could be printed on paper or projected onto a screen.

Sung worship acts as background music to prayer.

Zone 4

Prayer Ministry

In a side room, or an area separate from the main church.

The church prayer ministry team offering prayer to members of the congregation for their spiritual journey, not only emergency physical or spiritual needs.

Zone 5

The Word

In a side room, or an area separate from the main church.

The lectionary readings taken from the International Children's Bible repeated at regular intervals.

Read aloud by a reader or played from a prepared recording.

Projected images and/or music could accompany the readings.

Zone 6

Evangelistic All-age Talk

In a side room, or an area separate from the main church.

5-7 minutes in duration given every 10 minutes.

Could include illustrations, stories, illusions and demonstrations.

Zone 7

Creativity Area

In a side room, or an area separate from the main church.

Resources provided for painting and/or plasticine modelling.

The resulting pieces of artwork could be displayed in the main part of church.

Final gathering

Welcome

Eucharistic Prayer

Communion (contemporary music CD playing in the background)

Concluding Prayer (said by the service leader or a written prayer said by all)

Hymn or Song

Blessing

The Peace (shared as people depart)

Drinks

Give away A small item relating to the theme of today's worship given to each member of the congregation as they leave the church. To act as a reminder for what they have gained from the service. E.g. a jigsaw piece to remind people that everyone has a part to play in the body of Christ.